Lexis Rex

French Crosswords

Level 2, Volume 1

Welcome to the Lexis Rex French Crossword series, specially created for new and intermediate French language students.

In this Level 2 volume there are 125 crosswords to keep you practiced in French vocabulary, all of the clues are given in English. We have chosen the words from a larger set of the most common French words than Level 1, more words, phrases and verb conjugations you will find useful to know as you build your French mastery.

Some notes about the clues: For verb conjugations, we give the personal pronoun in parenthesis in the English clue to indicate the inflection of the answer. For the case of the English *you* we also show the appropriate French pronoun for the various cases, e.g. *(you/tu)* or *(you/vous)*. For the verb tenses, we have limited the modes to the indicative and the conditional, and we use a regular form for the English clues to indicate which tense. So for example you will find clues for the present tense verb *vais, (I) go*, the past imperfect *allais, (I) was going* or *(I) used to go*, the future *irai, (I) will go*, and the conditional *irais, (I) would go*. You will also find the present participle *allant* (going), and the past participle *allé* (went).

There are also common French phrases (the clue will show the number of letters in each word of the phrase), plurals and in some cases the clue will indicate that the feminine version of a word is required.

We hope you enjoy our crosswords, a great way to challenge your French knowledge and discover new words.

Published by Lexis Rex Language Books
Brisbane, Australia
support@lexisrex.com

ISBN 978-0-9942082-5-5

No. 1

1 A	■	2 M	E	3 R	C	4 R	E	5 D	I
6 F	É	E	■	Â	■	I	■	U	■
F	■	7 T	Ô	T	■	8 T	9 I	R	10 E
11 I	L	S	■	E	■	■	R	■	N
R	■	■	■	12 A	13 S	S	A	U	T
14 M	A	15 N	Q	U	E	■	■	■	E
E	■	O	■	■	R	■	16 S	O	N
17 R	18 E	N	19 D	■	20 O	I	E	■	D
■	A	■	O	■	N	■	21 R	U	E
22 A	U	S	S	I	T	Ô	T	■	Z

Across

2. day of the week
6. fairy
7. early
8. *(I)* shoot, draw
11. they
12. assault
14. a lack
16. his, her, its sound
17. *(he, she)* makes, renders
20. goose
21. street, road
22. immediately

Down

1. to affirm
2. *(I)* put
3. rake
4. *(he, she)* laughs
5. hard
9. *(he, she)* will go
10. *(you/vous)* hear
13. *(they)* will be
15. no
16. *(he, she)* serves
18. water
19. back

fairy = fée (f)

assault = assaut (m)

goose = oie (f)

rake = râteau (m)

serves = sert

No. 2

1 V	O	2 U	D	R	3 A		4 F	I	5 L
I		N			V		A		I
6 N	A	I	S	S	A	N	C	E	S
		V			L		I		A
7 P	I	E	R	8 R	E		L		I
O		R		9 A	R	G	E	N	T
U		S		I			M		
10 L	A	I	S	S	A	I	E	N	11 T
E		T		I			N		U
12 T	H	É		13 N	A	Î	T	R	E

Across

1. *(he, she)* will want
4. thread, wire
6. births
7. stone
9. silver
10. *(they)* were leaving *(behind)*
12. tea
13. to be born

Down

1. wine
2. college, university
3. to swallow
4. easily, readily
5. *(he, she)* was reading
7. chicken
8. grape
11. *(I)* kill

thread/wire = fil (m)

No. 3

Across

1. some, a little
5. fire
6. sole plant
8. altar
9. obscure, dim
12. poetry
14. a little, a bit *(2,3)*
15. to reign
17. heap, pile
18. cosmos

Down

1. left, departed
2. job, employment
3. quays, docks
4. *(he, she)* is east
5. to hit, strike
7. faults
10. butter
11. hoods
13. felt
16. elected

No. 4

■	■	1 A	R	2 R	A	3 C	H	4 É	■
5 S	U	R	■	É	■	E	■	M	■
O	■	6 M	E	S	■	7 S	8 Œ	U	9 R
10 U	N	E	■	E	■	■	I	■	I
R	■	■	■	11 A	12 S	I	L	E	S
13 C	H	14 A	Q	U	E	■	■	■	Q
I	■	M	■	■	M	■	15 P	L	U
16 L	17 O	I	18 N	■	19 B	A	L	■	E
■	N	■	O	■	L	■	20 A	I	R
■	21 T	O	M	B	E	N	T	■	■

Across

1. uprooted, pulled up, torn out
5. above, on top
6. put, placed
7. sister
10. a, an *(fem)*
11. asylums
13. each, every
15. pleased
    rained
16. far, distant
19. ball
20. appearance, look
21. *(they)* fall

Down

1. weapon
2. net, network
3. these
4. *(emotionally)* touched, moved
5. eyebrow
8. eye
9. to risk
12. *(it)* seems
14. friend
15. flat
17. *(they)* have
18. name

uprooted = arraché

asylums = asiles (m)

net = réseau (m)

touched = ému

No. 5

Across

1. shampoo
6. beaten
7. hand
8. to stay
   to remain
10. examination
13. she
14. *(I)* will have
15. thirty one *(6,2,2)*

Down

1. suddenly
2. act
   action
3. poor
4. *(he, she)* would go
5. generation
9. opposite *(2,4)*
11. driveway
12. finished, ready

beaten = battu

exam = examen (m)

suddenly = subitement

driveway = allée (f.)

No. 6

1 P	A	2 R	■	3 S	O	M	4 M	E	5 T
O	■	É	■	E	■	■	A	■	O
6 M	E	C	A	N	I	C	I	E	N
M	■	O	■	T	■	■	N	■	■
E	■	M	■	7 I	8 M	I	T	E	9 R
10 S	E	P	A	R	É	■	E	■	E
■	■	E	■	■	P	■	N	■	N
11 C	O	N	C	E	R	N	A	N	T
O	■	S	■	■	I	■	N	■	R
12 L	U	E	U	R	S	■	13 T	U	É

Across

1. by, by means of
   at the rate of, per
3. summit, peak
6. mechanic
7. to mimic, copy
10. separated
11. concerning, regarding
12. glows
13. killed

Down

1. apples
2. reward
3. to smell
   to feel
4. at present, now
5. your
8. scorn, contempt
9. re-entered, went back
11. collar

glows = lueurs (f)

reward = récompense (f)

Scorn = mépris (m)

No. 7

Across

1. *(I)* know
3. according to; depending on
6. pondered, reflected
9. six
10. certain, sure
11. opinion advice
13. motorcycle
14. painting, theatre, music etc
16. believed raw
17. spectacles
20. enough quite
21. *(I)* lift

Down

1. *(you)* will be
2. floor
3. dry
4. leaving
5. nut
7. formulas
8. state, condition
12. way, track
15. cup
16. that, that over there
18. nose
19. such

No. 8

1 P	2 R	O	3 F	O	4 N	D			5 R
	U		[illegible]		A		6 F	O	I
	7 E	8 N	L	E	V	E	R		V
9 À		A			I		10 O	U	I
11 S	O	R	T	12 I	R		T		È
A		I		13 M	E	N	T	I	R
14 V	I	N		P			E		E
O		15 E	N	O	U	16 T	R	17 E	
18 I	L	S		S		O		A	
R			19 S	É	R	I	E	U	X

Across

1. deep
6. faith
7. to remove, take off
10. yes
11. to go out, exit
13. to lie
14. wine
15. besides, moreover, furthermore *(2,5)*
18. they
19. serious

Down

2. street, road
3. thread, wire
4. ship
5. river
6. to rub
8. nostrils
9. namely, to wit *(1,6)*
12. imposed
16. you
17. water

besides = en outre

ship = navire (m)

namely = à savoir

No. 9

1 L	I	2 S	A	I	3 T	■	4 C	A	5 S
A	■	I	■	■	R	■	A	■	E
6 C	O	M	P	T	E	R	S	U	R
■	■	P	■	■	N	■	S	■	A
7 S	O	L	D	8 A	T	■	E	■	I
O	■	E	■	9 V	E	R	R	A	S
N	■	M	■	I	■	■	O	■	■
10 G	R	E	N	O	U	I	L	L	11 E
E	■	N	■	N	■	■	E	■	S
12 R	I	T	■	13 S	A	I	S	I	T

Across

1. *(he, she)* was reading
4. case, instance
6. to count on, rely on *(7,3)*
7. soldier
9. *(you)* will see
10. frog
12. *(he, she)* laughs
13. *(he, she)* seizes

Down

1. lake
2. simply
3. thirty
4. saucepans
5. *(you)* would be
7. to think about, ponder
8. airplanes
11. *(he, she)* is
    east

seizes = saisit

ponder = songer

No. 10

Across

1. enchanted, delighted
7. life
8. bitter, sour
9. title
10. locker
13. to tighten; to shake *(hands)*
15. husbands
16. ardour
18. law
19. to resist

Down

2. name
3. bold, courageous, daring
4. to be born
5. to avoid
6. to live, stay, remain
8. accomplished, finished
11. to serve
12. tests, trials
14. wrinkles
17. a, an *(fem)*

No. 11

Across

1. teardrops
4. hard
6. moments
9. early
10. rained
    pleased
11. evening
13. nothing
14. years
15. here
16. to accept
20. clear, distinct
21. *(I)* will know

Down

1. *(to)* him/her
2. *(he, she)* puts
3. his, her, its
    sound
4. distracted, absent-minded
5. *(you)* remain
7. smiling
8. ease
10. jail
12. eleven
17. these
18. not much, little
19. king

teardrops = larmes (f)

clear = net

ease = aise (f)

No. 12

■	■	1 D	I	2 S	C	3 R	E	4 T	■
5 S	U	R	■	A	■	E	■	U	■
O	■	O	■	6 M	O	N	T	E	7 R
8 R	E	I	N	E	■	D	■	■	I
T	■	T	■	9 D	10 E	S	11 S	U	S
12 A	V	E	13 N	I	R	■	I	■	Q
I	■	■	U	■	14 R	O	M	P	U
15 T	16 I	M	I	D	E	■	P	■	E
■	R	■	T	■	U	■	17 L	A	S
■	18 A	B	S	U	R	D	E	■	■

Across

1. discreet
5. above, on top
6. to climb
8. queen
9. on top of
12. the future
14. broken
15. shy
17. tired, weary
18. crazy

Down

1. *(on the)* right
2. day of the week
3. *(I)* render
4. *(I)* kill
5. *(he, she)* was going out
7. perils, dangers
10. error
    mistake
11. easy, not complicated
    (ticket, room) single
13. nights
16. *(he, she)* will go

tired = las

crazy = absurde

No. 13

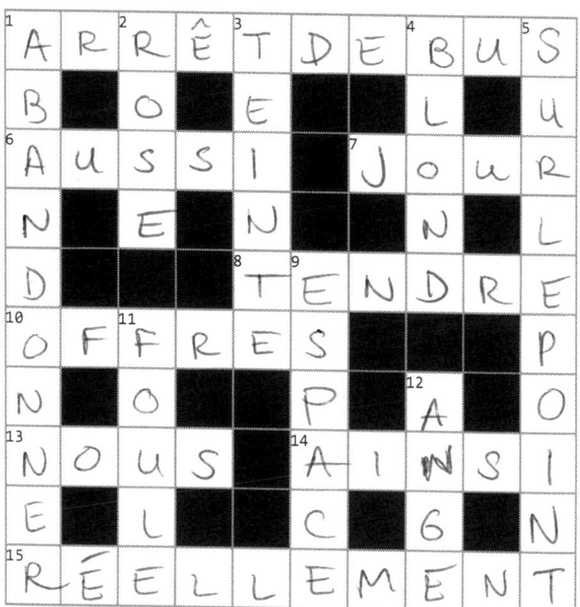

Across

1. bus stop *(5,2,3)*
6. too, also, as well
7. day
8. to stretch out, extend
   to tighten
10. *(you/tu)* offer
13. we
14. so, such, thereby, thus
15. actually, really

Down

1. to abandon, forsake
   to give up
2. pink
3. shade, tint
4. fair, fair-haired
5. on the brink *(of)*, on the verge *(of)* *(3,2,5)*
9. room, space
11. crowd
12. angel

stretch out = tendre

actually = réellement

shade = teinte (f)

on the brink = sur le point

No. 14

Across

1. passports
6. there are, there is *(2,1,1)*
7. felt
8. troop
10. arabs
13. wanted, desired
14. *(he, she)* will say
15. exactly

Down

1. point of view *(5,2,3)*
2. pen
3. to cross, go through, get over
   to pass
4. row
5. seizing
9. packet
11. to drink
12. *(he, she)* will have

row = rang (m)

seizing = saisissant

No. 15

1 A	O	Û	2 T	■	3 C	A	4 N	A	5 L
V	■	■	O	■	R	■	O	■	U
6 A	U	7 M	I	8 L	I	E	U	■	X
I	■	O	■	I	■	■	9 V	U	E
10 T	O	N	■	11 R	12 I	V	E	■	■
■	■	13 T	U	E	R	■	14 L	A	15 C
16 S	Û	R	■	■	A	■	L	■	Ô
E	■	17 A	R	18 R	I	19 V	E	N	T
I	■	I	■	U	■	I	■	■	E
20 N	O	T	R	E	■	21 F	A	I	S

Across

1. month of the year
3. artificial waterway
6. in the middle *(2,6)*
9. sight, view
10. your
11. bank *(of a river)*
13. to kill
14. lake
16. certain, sure
17. *(they)* arrive
20. our
21. *(I)* do

Down

1. *(he, she)* was having
2. you
3. shout, scream
4. new *(fem)*
5. luxury
7. *(he, she)* was showing
8. to read
12. *(I)* will go
15. coasts; ribs
16. bosom, breast
18. street, road
19. lively; vivid

breast = sein (m)

No. 16

Across

1. sea
3. threat
6. *(they)* were missing
7. worries
10. to tempt
    to try
11. character *(in a play, program, film)*
12. exit, way out
13. such

Down

1. short period of time
2. to meet, to come across
3. froth, foam; moss
4. *(he, she)* was glimpsing
5. *(he, she)* is
   east
8. a citrus fruit
9. sun
11. footstep
    not

threat = menace (f)

worries = souci (m)

froth = mousse (f)

glimpsing = apercevait

No. 17

Across

1. army
4. but
6. *(he, she)* would be able to
9. because, since
10. notion
12. dared
13. *(I)* live
    (you/tu) live
14. tire
15. king
17. brain
20. she
21. piece of writing

Down

1. with
2. to despise, scorn
3. water
4. wall
5. situated
7. nothing
8. in love, amorous
11. sword
13. cow
16. drunk, drunken, intoxicated
18. life
19. bed

brain = cervelle (F) | despise = mépriser

No. 18

Across

1. sock
6. *(I)* will have
7. high
   top
8. to write
10. to enter
13. *(I)* shoot, draw
14. picture
15. towels

Down

1. *(horse drawn)* carts
2. shelter
3. evening
4. betrayed
5. interviews
9. to believe, to think
11. to draw, drag, pull
    to shoot
12. milk

cart = charette (f)

shelter = abri (m)

betrayed = trahi

interview = entretien (m)

No. 19

1 P	2 L	E	3 U	R	4 A	N	5 T	■	6 E
■	O	■	N	■	S	■	7 A	N	S
8 A	I	9 S	E	■	10 S	O	N	■	P
P	■	U	■	■	U	■	11 T	H	É
12 P	A	R	L	13 E	R	■	■	■	R
E	■	■	■	14 M	E	T	15 T	R	A
16 L	I	17 É	■	P	■	■	U	■	I
A	■	18 G	E	L	■	19 V	E	20 N	T
21 I	R	A	■	O	■	A	■	O	■
T	■	22 L	A	I	S	S	E	N	T

Across

1. crying
7. years
8. ease
10. his, her, its sound
11. tea
12. to speak
14. *(he, she)* will put
16. linked
18. frost
19. wind
21. *(he, she)* will go
22. *(they)* leave

Down

2. law
3. a, an *(fem)*
4. *(I)* make sure
5. so much, so many
6. *(he, she)* was hoping
8. *(he, she)* was calling
9. above, on top
13. job, employment
15. *(I)* kill
17. equal, even, level
19. *(you)* go
20. no

linked = lié

frost = gel (m)

equal = égal

No. 20

Across

1. to find
6. end
   fine
7. playhouse
10. clear, distinct
11. *(he, she)* was reading
13. chin
14. word
15. entries
18. hard
19. troubled

Down

2. *(he, she)* laughs
3. used
   worn *(out, down)*
4. ahead; in the lead *(2,4)*
5. moment
6. window
8. to hesitate
9. fashionable *(1,2,4)*
12. to mimic, copy
16. elected
17. salt

No. 21

1 A	R	2 R	Ê	3 T	D	E	4 B	U	5 S
B	■	A	■	R	■	■	L	■	U
6 A	N	N	É	E	■	7 P	O	U	R
N	■	G	■	N	■	■	N	■	L
D	■	■	■	8 T	9 E	N	D	R	E
10 O	F	11 F	R	E	S	■	■	■	P
N	■	E	■	■	P	■	12 A	■	O
13 N	O	M	S	■	14 A	I	N	S	I
E	■	M	■	■	C	■	G	■	N
15 R	É	E	L	L	E	M	E	N	T

Across

1. bus stop *(5,2,3)*
6. year
7. for, to
8. to tighten
   to stretch out, extend
10. *(you/tu)* offer
13. names
14. so, such, thereby, thus
15. actually, really

Down

1. to abandon, forsake
   to give up
2. row
3. thirty
4. fair, fair-haired
5. on the brink *(of)*, on the verge *(of)* *(3,2,5)*
9. room, space
11. woman
12. angel

No. 22

Across

1. compass point
3. hours
6. to interest
7. effects
10. amount, number
11. to advise, to counsel
12. *(you)* would be
13. street, road

Down

1. season
2. to determine, establish
3. to shout
4. to resemble
5. certain, sure
8. *(you/vous)* would do, make
9. origin, spring
11. these

shout = hurler

origin = source (f)

No. 23

■	■	1 É	T	2 A	B	3 L	I	4 T	■
5 L	I	T	■	N	■	I	■	O	■
A	■	6 A	M	I	■	7 S	8 O	I	9 E
10 V	I	T	■	M	■	■	I	■	N
E	■	■	■	11 A	12 R	G	E	N	T
13 R	E	14 M	P	L	I	■	■	■	E
I	■	A	■	■	S	■	15 B	O	N
16 E	17 L	L	18 E	■	19 Q	U	E	■	D
■	A	■	A	■	U	■	20 C	A	S
■	21 S	O	U	P	E	R	S	■	■

Across

1. *(he, she)* establishes
5. bed
6. friend
7. silk
10. *(he, she)* lives
11. silver
13. filled
15. good
16. she
19. that
20. case, instance
21. suppers

Down

1. state, condition
2. beast
3. *(I)* read
4. you
5. laundry
8. goose
9. *(you/tu)* hear
   (I) hear
12. risk
14. bad, wrong
    pain
15. beaks, bills
17. tired, weary
18. water

Supper = souper (m)

laundry = laverie (f)
goose = oie (f)
tired = las

No. 24

Across

1. sculptures
5. *(they)* have
6. calls
8. according to; depending on
9. to run
12. to stay
    to remain
14. dignified
15. lightning
17. *(he, she)* is
    east
18. to leave

Down

1. pens
2. advance
3. a little, a bit *(2,3)*
4. floor
5. observed
7. *(they)* serve
10. orders
11. to sort out, to settle
    to set, to adjust
13. betrayed
16. collar

No. 25

Across

1. *(he, she)* was beating
5. years
7. *(have)* gone
9. his, her, its sound
10. such
11. resolved
13. established
15. lively; vivid
17. *(he, she)* will go
18. folds
20. they, them
21. asleep

Down

1. bowl
2. tea
3. assault
4. so much, so many
6. suns
7. arrival
8. the *(plural)*
12. lizard
14. ball
16. *(I)* fix, fasten
18. by, by means of at the rate of, per
19. here

No. 26

Across

1. scarf
5. clear, distinct
7. nearby
8. traced
9. to believe, to think
12. appearance, look facet, angle
14. dreams
15. *(I)* occupy *(he, she)* occupies
17. above, on top
18. horror

Down

1. elected
2. bold, courageous, daring
3. *(you)* remain
4. opposite *(2,4)*
6. playhouse
7. agreements
10. open
11. razor
13. pocket
16. pure

nearby = auprès

bold = hardi

razor = rasoir (m)

No. 27

Across

1. late
3. fair, fair-haired
6. pianist
9. they
10. dry
11. equal, even, level
13. to dare
14. lake
16. name
17. to procure
20. broken, destroyed
21. sword

Down

1. carpet
2. gift
3. low
4. pillow
5. *(I)* must
7. accomplished, finished
8. notion
12. Greek
15. card
map
16. black
18. dared
19. used
worn *(out, down)*

No. 28

1 R	E	2 P	U	B	3 L	I	4 Q	U	5 E
E	■	E	■	■	E	■	U	■	N
6 C	E	N	T	■	7 Q	U	A	R	T
I	■	D	■	■	U	■	I	■	R
8 P	O	U	S	9 S	E	■	■	■	E
I	■	■	■	10 A	L	L	11 A	I	T
E	■	12 B	■	M	■	■	V	■	I
13 N	E	I	G	E	■	14 M	I	N	E
T	■	E	■	D	■	■	O	■	N
15 S	E	N	T	I	M	E	N	T	S

Across

1. republic
6. hundred
7. fourth, quarter
8. sprout, growth
10. *(he, she)* was going
13. snow
14. mineral excavation
15. feelings

Down

1. containers
2. hanged
3. which, that, whom
4. quay
5. interviews
9. day of the week
11. airplane
12. well

growth = pousse (f)

min. excav = mine (f)

hanged = pendu

No. 29

Across

1. season
4. word
6. to determine, establish
7. to speak
9. novels
10. *(they)* start
12. *(emotionally)* touched, moved
13. re-entered, went back

Down

1. compass point
2. interrupted
3. issue, number
4. *(they)* were missing
5. terms
7. leaning
8. error mistake
11. killed

novel = roman (m)

touched = ému

interrupted = interrompu

leaning = penché

No. 30

■	■	1 D	É	2 F	E	3 N	S	4 E	■
5 P	E	U	■	A	■	O	■	S	■
I	■	6 R	O	I	■	7 N	8 O	T	9 E
10 L	I	É	■	B	■	■	U	■	N
O	■	■	■	11 L	12 A	P	I	N	S
13 T	O	14 M	B	E	R	■	■	■	U
É	■	O	■	■	B	■	15 L	U	I
16 S	17 O	I	18 F	■	19 R	U	E	■	T
■	N	■	O	■	E	■	20 U	N	E
■	21 T	O	U	S	S	E	R	■	■

Across

1. prohibition defence
5. not much, little
6. king
7. short written message
10. linked
11. rabbits
13. to fall
15. *(to)* him/her
16. thirst
19. street, road
20. a, an *(fem)*
21. to cough

Down

1. lasted
2. weak
3. no
4. *(he, she)* is east
5. pilots
8. yes
9. subsequently, next
12. trees
14. me
15. their
17. *(they)* have
18. mad

✓

No. 31

Across

1. loves, passions
4. *(he, she)* lives
6. to collect, gather
7. opposed
9. texts
10. actually, really
12. *(he, she)* laughs
13. *(he, she)* seizes

Down

1. appearance, look
2. *(they)* were occupying
3. evening
4. willingly, gladly
5. tyrants
7. to open
8. pens
11. early

collect = récueiller | willingly = volontiers

No. 32

1 É	L	È	2 V	È	3 S	■	4 D	U	5 R
T	■	■	I	■	U	■	E	■	E
6 É	P	7 I	N	8 A	R	D	S	■	D
■	■	N	■	G	■	■	9 C	O	U
10 C	A	S	■	11 I	12 V	R	E	■	I
L	■	13 T	I	R	E	■	14 N	E	T
15 I	R	A	■	■	U	■	D	■	■
M	■	16 L	E	17 C	T	18 E	U	R	19 S
A	■	L	■	E	■	A	■	■	Û
20 T	H	É	■	21 S	A	U	V	E	R

Across

1. students
4. hard
6. spinach
9. neck
10. case, instance
11. drunk, drunken, intoxicated
13. *(I)* shoot, draw
14. clear, distinct
15. *(he, she)* will go
16. readers
20. tea
21. to save

Down

1. season of the year
2. wine
3. above, on top
4. descended
5. reduced
7. installed
8. to act
10. climate
12. *(he, she)* wants
17. these
18. water
19. certain, sure

neck = cou (m)
clear = net

reduced = reduit
to act = agir

No. 33

Across

1. *(they)* present
6. so that, in order that
7. to steal
   to fly
8. to marry
10. *(he, she)* would do, make
13. picture
14. true
    real
15. necessary, needful

Down

1. pharmacist
2. sink, basin
3. ship
4. she
5. territory, turf
9. effects
11. *(I)* will have
12. bench

So that = afin

marry = marier

sink = évier (m)

bench = banc (m)

No. 34

Across

1. despite, in spite of, notwithstanding
4. his, her, its
   sound
6. to indicate
9. by, by means of
   at the rate of, per
10. put, placed
11. to dare
13. a *(female)* friend
14. here
15. you
16. *(they)* exist
20. painting, theatre, music etc
21. rooms

Down

1. month of the year
2. cheerful
   gay
3. elected
4. something unexpected
5. fed
7. *(they)* were saying
8. what
10. *(he, she)* will put
12. meaning
17. they
18. such
19. heap, pile

No. 35

1 N	2 O	V	3 E	M	4 B	R	5 E	■	6 E
■	I	■	N	■	A	■	7 M	O	N
8 S	E	N	T	■	L	■	P	■	C
A	■	■	R	■	9 C	A	L	M	E
10 N	U	11 M	É	12 R	O	■	O	■	I
G	■	O	■	13 A	N	14 C	I	E	N
15 L	A	M	E	S	■	A	■	■	T
O	■	E	■	16 O	C	C	U	17 P	E
18 T	O	N	■	U	■	H	■	U	■
S	■	19 T	E	R	R	E	U	R	S

Across

1. month of the year
7. my
8. *(he, she)* smells
9. calm
10. issue, number
13. old, former, ex-
15. blades
16. *(I)* occupy *(he, she)* occupies
18. your
19. terrors

Down

2. goose
3. entered
4. balcony
5. job, employment
6. pregnant
8. sobs
11. short period of time
12. razor
14. hiding place
17. pure

blade = lame (f)

pregnant = enceinte

sobs = sanglot (m)

razor = rasoir (m)

1	■	2		3		4		5	
6			■		■		■		■
	■		■		■	7			8
9					■		■	■	
	■		■	10	11		12		
13			14			■		■	
	■	■		■	15				
16	17					■		■	
■		■		■		■	18		
19								■	

Across

2. pleasant, pleasing
6. sight, view
7. glove
9. tablecloth
10. path, way
13. warned, averted
15. your
16. respect, regard
18. iron
19. addresses

Down

1. advantage
2. people *(of a nation)*
3. appearance, look
   facet, angle
4. sign, signal
5. no
8. thunder
11. winters
12. patterns
14. queen
17. compass point

1 A	V	E	2 U	■	3 Q	U	4 A	N	5 D
V	■	■	N	■	U	■	U	■	E
6 R	Ê	7 V	E	8 R	I	E	S	■	U
I	■	O	■	I	■	■	9 S	I	X
10 L	U	I	■	11 R	12 A	V	I	■	■
■	■	13 T	U	E	R	■	14 T	U	15 É
16 P	E	U	■	■	M	■	Ô	■	L
E	■	17 R	E	18 M	E	19 T	T	R	E
R	■	E	■	U	■	Ô	■	■	V
20 D	É	S	I	R	■	21 T	I	R	É

Across

1. confession, admission
3. when
6. daydreams
9. six
10. *(to)* him/her
11. thrilled, delighted
13. to kill
14. killed
16. not much, little
17. to put back
20. wish
21. drawn, dragged shot

Down

1. month of the year
2. a, an *(fem)*
3. who
4. immediately
5. two
7. cars
8. to laugh
12. weapon
15. high; raised
16. *(he, she)* loses
18. wall
19. early

confession = aveu (m)

No. 38

Across

1. *(we)* will have
4. *(I)* live
   (you/tu) live
6. to collect, gather
7. to fall
9. to smell
   to feel
10. *(they)* were showing
12. season of the year
13. sad

Down

1. appearance, look
2. recommended
3. to follow
4. willingly, gladly
5. to tighten; to shake *(hands)*
7. deceived
8. spirit; mind
11. *(I)* kill

No. 39

1 M	2 O	U	3 T	A	4 R	D	5 E	■	6 D
■	U	■	E	■	I	■	7 F	É	E
8 H	I	E	R	■	S	■	F	■	M
O	■	■	R	■	9 Q	U	E	U	E
10 N	I	11 V	E	12 A	U	■	T	■	U
N	■	A	■	13 V	E	14 R	S	E	R
15 E	N	C	R	E	■	O	■	■	E
U	■	H	■	16 N	O	M	M	17 E	R
18 R	U	E	■	I	■	A	■	A	■
S	■	19 S	Y	R	I	N	G	U	E

Across

1. mustard
7. fairy
8. yesterday
9. tail
10. level
13. to pour
15. ink
16. to name
18. street, road
19. syringe

Down

2. yes
3. earth
4. risk
5. effects
6. to live, stay, remain
8. honors
11. cows
12. the future
14. novel
17. water

tail = queue (f)

pour = verser

ink = encre (f)

No. 40

P	U	I	S	S	A	N	C	E	S
O		M			V		E		A
I	R	A	I		A	V	R	A	I
N		G			L		F		S
T	R	E	N	T	E				I
D				A	R	A	B	E	S
E		S		N			A		A
V	I	E	N	T		I	L	Y	A
U		R		Ô			L		N
E	X	A	C	T	E	M	E	N	T

Across

1. powers
6. *(I)* will go
7. *(I)* will have
8. thirty
10. arabs
13. *(he, she)* comes
14. there are, there is *(2,1,1)*
15. exactly

Down

1. point of view *(5,2,3)*
2. picture
3. to swallow
4. deer
5. seizing
9. sometimes
11. bullet
ball
12. *(he, she)* will be

power = puissance (f)

deer = cerf (m)

seizing = saisisant

sometimes = tantôt

No. 41

1		2	■	3			4		5
	■		■		■	■		■	
6									
	■		■		■	■		■	■
	■		■	7	8				9
10						■		■	
■	■		■	■		■		■	
11									
	■		■	■		■		■	
12						■	13		

Across

1. certain, sure
3. threat
6. rapidly
7. *(he, she)* walks
   (I) walk
10. rooms
11. make-up
12. glows
13. you

Down

1. *(we)* will be
2. republic
3. form of address for a woman, Mrs or Ms
4. *(he, she)* was glimpsing
5. *(he, she)* is
   east
8. asylums
9. foe
11. bad, wrong
    pain

No. 42

Across

1. anxieties
7. believed
   raw
8. committed, engaged
10. clear, distinct
11. salt
13. notion
15. ease
16. above, on top
17. month of the year
18. atrocious
21. *(I)* read
22. *(it)* had being

Down

2. no
3. *(he, she)* will go
4. tea
5. *(theatre)* stages
6. fourteen
8. together
9. grey
12. *(he, she)* leaves *(behind)*
    (I) leave *(behind)*
14. tooth
18. friend
19. *(he, she)* laughs
20. shout, scream

atrocious = atroce
it had being = exister

shout = crier

No. 43

1 c	o	2 n	v	3 a	i	n	4 c	r	5 e
a		u		r			h		n
6 p	r	i	e	r		7 l	a	i	t
i		t		ê			u		r
t				8 t	9 e	n	d	r	e
10 a	n	11 c	i	e	n				t
i		r			f		12 é		i
13 n	o	i	x		14 a	u	t	r	e
e		e			c		a		n
15 s	e	r	v	i	e	t	t	e	s

Across

1. to convince
6. to pray
7. milk
8. to tighten
   to stretch out, extend
10. old, former, ex-
13. nut
14. other, another
15. towels

Down

1. captains
2. night
3. *(he, she)* stops
   (I) stop
4. hot
5. interviews
9. opposite *(2,4)*
11. to scream
12. state, condition

pray = prier | interview = entretien (m)

No. 44

Across

1. freedom
5. name
7. curtain
8. dictator, despot
9. hunt
12. appearance, look
    facet, angle
14. on fire, ablaze *(2,3)*
15. sad
17. his, her, its
    sound
18. furthermore, besides, on top of that *(2,5)*

Down

1. *(to)* him/her
2. goods
3. roads, highways
4. enormous
6. monster
7. rocks
10. deep down, at bottom, at the end *(2,4)*
11. to jump, leap
13. weight
16. *(I)* kill

furthermore = du reste

No. 45

Across

1. favorites
5. worn *(out, down)* used
7. more
9. me
10. killed
11. the future
13. limb, member
15. floor
17. *(they)* have
18. flat
20. king
21. surprised

Down

1. thread, wire
2. *(you/tu)* live *(I)* live
3. to break
4. *(he, she)* follows
6. element
7. pleasure
8. a, an *(fem)*
12. to mimic, copy
14. bowl
16. laws
18. by, by means of at the rate of, per
19. years

No. 46

Across

1. inspired
5. because, since
6. appearance, look
7. sister
10. here
11. job, employment
13. dark
15. yes
16. lot, fate
    (he, she) goes out
19. your
20. dice
21. petrol

Down

1. *(I)* will go
2. to tighten; to shake *(hands)*
3. they
4. elected
5. thighs
8. eye
9. grapes
12. chin
14. sea
15. wave
17. goose
18. heap, pile

No. 47

Across

1. *(I)* say
   (you/tu) say
3. whole, entire
6. fork
7. razor
10. terms
11. to construct, build
12. glows
13. water

Down

1. fault, defect
2. suffering
3. again
   still, yet
4. to introduce
5. street, road
8. stars
9. net, network
11. collar

No. 48

1 P	A	2 R	F	U	3 M	■	4 L	I	5 É
A	■	E	■	■	E	■	A	■	T
6 S	E	C	R	E	T	A	I	R	E
■	■	O	■	■	T	■	S	■	I
7 T	O	M	B	8 E	R	■	S	■	N
R	■	M	■	9 S	E	R	A	I	T
O	■	A	■	P	■	■	I	■	■
10 M	O	N	T	R	A	I	E	N	11 T
P	■	D	■	I	■	■	N	■	Ô
12 É	T	É	■	13 T	A	N	T	Ô	T

Across

1. perfume
4. linked
6. secretary
7. to fall
9. *(he, she)* would
10. *(they)* were showing
12. season of the year
13. sometimes

Down

1. footstep
not
2. recommended
3. to put
4. *(they)* were leaving *(behind)*
5. extinct
extinguished, out
7. deceived
8. spirit; mind
11. early

extinct = éteint

No. 49

Across

1. these
3. faults
6. to consider
7. rabbits
10. to name
11. fantasies
12. tried
13. *(he, she)* is east

Down

1. pig
2. feelings
3. weak
4. territory, turf
5. above, on top
8. arrived
9. *(he, she)* seizes
11. fairy

No. 50

■	1 S	O	2 M	M	3 E	I	4 L	■	■
■	Û	■	A	■	S	■	5 A	M	6 I
7 P	R	E	N	D	S	■	V	■	N
A	■	■	G	■	8 A	V	A	N	T
9 S	A	10 M	E	11 D	I	■	B	■	E
S	■	I	■	12 E	S	13 P	O	I	R
14 A	P	R	È	S	■	O	■	■	Ê
N	■	O	■	15 S	E	R	O	16 N	T
17 T	O	I	■	U	■	T	■	E	■
■	■	18 R	E	S	P	E	C	T	■

Across

1. sleep
5. friend
7. *(I)* take
8. before
9. day of the week
12. hope
14. after
15. *(they)* will be
17. you
18. consideration

Down

1. certain, sure
2. *(I)* eat
   (he, she) eats
3. tests, trials
4. sink
6. interest
7. passing
10. mirror
11. on top of
13. *(I)* wear
    (I) carry
16. clear, distinct

consideration = respect (m)

No. 51

Across

1. engineers
6. tight, taught
7. movie
8. alarm clock
10. actually; in fact *(really)* (2,4)
13. minus, without
14. snow
15. *(he, she)* was finding *(again)*

Down

1. to interest
2. glove
3. fed
4. useful
5. simply
9. extensive; widespread
11. *(he, she)* finishes
12. *(he, she)* will say

extensive = étendu

No. 52

Across

1. remorse
5. mad
6. size
   waist
9. *(he, she)* will go
10. short written message
12. bed
13. years
14. *(I)* will go
15. my
16. *(we)* are
20. heap, pile
21. strange

Down

1. ribbons
2. word
3. king
4. salt
5. *(you/tu)* were doing, making
   (I) was doing, making
7. bitter, sour
8. *(you/tu)* hear
   (I) hear
11. *(I)* shoot, draw
12. outer bound
17. dared
18. sea
19. his, her, its
    sound

remorse = remords (m)

ribbon = ruban (m)

No. 53

Across

1. walks
6. *(you)* have
7. sold
8. job, profession
10. to close, shut
13. picture
14. brown
15. necessary, needful

Down

1. pharmacist
2. compass point
3. ship
4. in
5. suffering
9. effects
11. day of the week
12. bench

No. 54

1 A	■	2 D	U	3 R	E	4 T	O	5 U	R
6 C	O	U	■	E	■	A	■	N	■
C	■	R	■	7 N	A	P	P	E	8 S
9 E	X	A	C	T	■	I	■	■	E
P	■	N	■	10 R	11 E	S	12 T	E	R
13 T	I	T	14 R	E	S	■	I	■	A
E	■	■	A	■	15 P	A	R	M	I
16 R	17 É	G	N	E	R	■	A	■	E
■	L	■	G	■	I	■	18 N	O	N
19 A	U	S	S	I	T	Ô	T	■	N

Across

2. back, returned *(2,6)*
6. neck
7. tablecloths
9. precise
10. to stay
    to remain
13. titles
15. among
16. to reign
18. no
19. immediately

Down

1. to accept
2. during
3. *(he, she)* goes back in
   (I) go back in
4. carpet
5. a, an *(fem)*
8. *(they)* would be
11. spirit; mind
12. drawing, dragging, pulling
    shooting
14. rows
17. elected

back = du retour

among = parmi

Across

1. disgust
4. footstep
not
6. to meet, to come across
7. to go out, exit
9. to lie
10. at present, now
12. your
13. re-entered, went back

Down

1. hard
2. generation
3. to stretch out, extend
to tighten
4. *(he, she)* used to allow
5. to serve
7. summit, peak
8. to mimic, copy
11. killed

disgust = dégout (m)

No. 56

1 C	E	2 S	■	3 M	É	P	4 R	I	5 S
O	■	E	■	O	■	■	É	■	U
6 C	O	N	D	U	I	T	E	U	R
H	■	T	■	S	■	■	L	■	■
O	■	I	■	7 S	8 A	L	L	E	9 S
10 N	O	M	M	E	R	■	E	■	O
■	■	E	■	■	G	■	M	■	R
11 F	I	N	A	L	E	M	E	N	T
I	■	T	■	■	N	■	N	■	I
12 L	I	S	A	I	T	■	13 T	U	E

Across

1. these
3. scorn, contempt
6. driver
7. rooms
10. to name
11. finally
12. *(he, she)* was reading
13. *(I)* kill

Down

1. pig
2. feelings
3. froth, foam; moss
4. actually, really
5. above, on top
8. silver
9. exit, way out
11. thread, wire

No. 57

1 A	■	2 P	R	3 E	S	4 S	I	5 O	N
6 G	A	I	■	S	■	E	■	U	■
I	■	E	■	T	■	7 N	O	I	8 R
9 S	E	R	A	I	■	T	■	■	E
S	■	R	■	10 M	11 A	I	12 S	O	N
13 A	M	E	14 N	E	R	■	E	■	T
I	■	■	U	■	15 D	Î	N	E	R
16 T	17 O	M	A	T	E	■	T	■	A
■	I	■	G	■	U	■	18 I	C	I
19 D	E	M	E	U	R	E	R	■	T

Across

2. pressure
6. cheerful
   gay
7. black
9. *(I)* will be
10. home
13. to bring
15. dinner
16. tomato
18. here
19. to live, stay, remain

Down

1. *(he, she)* was acting
2. stone
3. respect, regard
4. felt
5. yes
8. *(he, she)* was going back in
11. ardour
12. to smell
    to feel
14. cloud
17. goose

pressure = pression (f)

No. 58

1 f	2 l	a	3 m	m	4 e	■	5 a	■	6 f
■	i	■	o	■	s	■	7 g	e	l
8 r	é	9 s	i	10 s	t	e	r	■	e
■	■	o	■	o	■	■	11 é	m	u
12 e	a	u	■	13 i	14 l	y	a	■	r
n	■	15 l	i	e	u	■	16 b	a	s
17 v	i	e	■	■	n	■	l	■	■
e	■	18 v	i	19 v	e	20 m	e	21 n	t
22 r	u	e	■	u	■	o	■	o	■
s	■	r	■	23 e	n	n	é	m	i

Across

1. flame
7. frost
8. to resist
11. *(emotionally)* touched, moved
12. water
13. there are, there is *(2,1,1)*
15. place
16. low
17. life
18. forcefully, vigorously
22. street, road
23. foe

Down

2. linked
3. me
4. *(he, she)* is
   east
5. agreeable, nice
6. flowers
9. to raise, to lift up, to pick up
10. silk
12. the reverse, back
    to, towards
14. moon
19. sight, view
20. my
21. name

No. 59

Across

1. to run
4. by, by means of at the rate of, per
6. seizing
7. *(I)* cry
9. tried
10. surgeries
12. season of the year
13. to ring, to sound

Down

1. case, instance
2. college, university
3. *(you)* remain
4. pharmacist
5. taken off, removed; withdrawn
7. leaning
8. reviews
11. certain, sure

takenoff = retiré

No. 60

1 A	P	2 P	A	R	3 E	N	4 C	E	5 S
S	■	E	■	■	S	■	H	■	U
6 C	E	R	F	■	7 P	L	O	M	B
E	■	D	■	■	R	■	U	■	I
8 N	O	U	R	9 R	I	■	■	■	T
S	■	■	■	10 É	T	O	11 I	L	E
E	■	12 F	■	V	■	■	M	■	M
13 U	T	I	L	E	■	14 F	A	C	E
R	■	L	■	I	■	■	G	■	N
15 S	I	M	P	L	E	M	E	N	T

Across

1. appearances
6. deer
7. lead
8. fed
10. star
13. useful
14. the front of the head, visage
15. simply

Down

1. lifts, elevators
2. lost
3. spirit; mind
4. cabbage
5. suddenly
9. alarm clock
11. picture
12. movie

appearance = apparence (f)

No. 61

Across

1. complaints
7. friend
8. son
10. month of the year
11. salt
12. *(I)* make sure
14. *(I)* get to, reach
16. footstep
    not
18. years
19. month of the year
21. no
22. sobs

Down

2. law
3. they
4. to fall
5. *(I)* know
6. thousands
8. striking
9. tired, weary
13. grape
15. *(he, she)* will go
17. minus, without
19. bad, wrong
    pain
20. *(he, she)* laughs

No. 62

1 R	E	2 C	U	E	3 I	L	4 L	E	5 R
É	■	R	■	■	N	■	O	■	É
6 P	E	U	X	■	7 F	A	I	R	E
U	■	E	■	■	I	■	N	■	L
8 B	A	L	L	9 O	N	■	■	■	L
L	■	■	■	10 F	I	È	11 V	R	E
I	■	12 S	■	F	■	■	O	■	M
13 Q	U	E	U	E	■	14 V	I	T	E
U	■	R	■	R	■	■	L	■	N
15 E	X	A	C	T	E	M	E	N	T

Across

1. to collect, gather
6. *(I)* can
7. to make
   to do
8. balloon
   football, soccer ball
10. fever
13. tail
14. quick, fast
15. exactly

Down

1. republic
2. not kind
3. endless
4. far, distant
5. actually, really
9. offered
11. veil
12. *(he, she)* will be

veil = voile (m)

No. 63

Across

1. cathedral
6. eager, greedy
7. finished, ready
8. ship
10. effects
13. held
14. envy
15. servants

Down

1. *(horse drawn)* carts
2. roof
3. extinguished, out extinct
4. *(I)* will have
5. interviews
9. appearance, look facet, angle
11. to end, complete
12. confession, admission

eager = avide

servant = serviteur (m)

Across

1. to appear *(become visible)*
6. *(he, she)* can
7. glimmer, glow
8. to stay
   to remain
10. *(he, she)* will put
13. altar
14. bench
15. territory, turf

Down

1. beforehand, previously
2. fears
3. speed, pace
   appearance, look
4. to kill
5. on the other hand *(2,8)*
9. job, employment
11. betrayed
12. to take away, remove

altar = autel (m)

beforehand = auparavant

o.t.o.h = en revanche

to remove = ôter

No. 65

Across

1. *(he, she)* was covering
7. painting, theatre, music etc
8. to tighten; to shake *(hands)*
9. driveway
10. even if *(4,2)*
    although, even though *(4,2)*
13. *(he, she)* waits, expects
15. day of the week
16. *(it)* seems
18. here
19. turned over, knocked over, spilt

Down

2. goose
3. glass
4. *(he, she)* would have
5. size
   waist
6. to wait for
   to expect
8. *(it)* seemed
11. to lie
12. season
14. grave
17. *(I)* read

No. 66

Across

1. more
3. *(I)* come
6. nobility
9. sea
10. above, on top
11. wolf
13. nothing
14. linked
16. fairy
17. to direct, address
20. piece of writing
21. night

Down

1. bridges
2. floor
3. *(you)* go
4. examples
5. evening
7. bars, rungs
8. she
12. eleven
15. *(he, she)* writes
16. fact
18. street, road
19. his, her, its sound

No. 67

Across

1. peril
4. by, by means of at the rate of, per
6. swiftness
9. compass point
10. tea
11. bank *(of a river)*
13. heaven, sky
14. nose
15. you
16. opposite *(2,4,2)*
20. six
21. net, network

Down

1. hard
2. cheerful gay
3. king
4. *(he, she)* presents *(I)* present
5. *(you/vous)* give back, return *(you/vous)* pay *(a visit)*
7. precious
8. to say, tell
10. titles
12. there are, there is *(2,1,1)*
17. iron
18. these
19. water

No. 68

Across

1. scholars
5. not much, little
6. *(he, she)* drank
   aim, goal
7. husband
10. me
11. spirit; mind
13. imposed
15. because, since
16. to laugh
19. friend
20. early
21. anxiety

Down

1. suffered, endured
2. window panes
3. name
4. certain, sure
5. fireman
8. appearance, look
9. interest
12. separated
14. pure
15. large town
17. *(he, she)* will go
18. they, them

No. 69

Across

1. to convince
6. tires
7. so much, so many
8. to render, make, pay *(a visit)*
10. old, former, ex-
13. black
14. asylum
15. servants

Down

1. captains
2. to deny
3. *(I)* make sure
4. hot
5. interviews
9. actually; in fact *(really)* (2,4)
11. to scream
12. god, deity

deny = nier

No. 70

1 D	O	2 S		3 C	O	U	4 S	I	5 N
U		É		A			A		O
6 M	É	C	A	N	A	C	I	E	N
Ê		R		A			S		
M		E		7 P	8 L	A	I	R	9 A
10 E	N	T	R	É	E		S		M
		A			Ç		S		I
11 C	L	I	G	N	O	T	A	N	T
O		R			N		N		I
12 L	U	E	U	R	S		13 T	U	É

Across

1. back
3. family relative
6. mechanic
7. *(it)* will please
10. entrance
11. indicator
12. glows
13. killed

Down

1. alike, equally, likewise *(2,4)*
2. secretary
3. sofa
4. seizing
5. no
8. lessons
9. friendship
11. collar

indicator = clignotant (m)

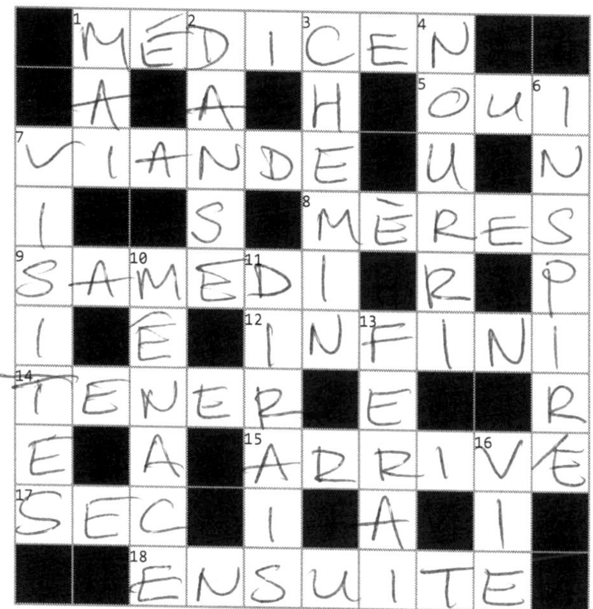

Across

1. medical doctor
5. yes
7. meat
8. mothers
9. day of the week
12. endless
14. to hold
to keep
15. arrived
17. dry
18. subsequently, next

Down

1. month of the year
2. dance
3. path, way
4. fed
6. inspired
7. social calls
10. threat
11. *(I)* would say
(you/tu) would say
13. *(I)* will do, make
16. life

No. 72

Across

1. *(they)* will do, make
4. case, instance
6. interrupted
7. froth, foam; moss
9. tests, trials
10. to work
12. clear, distinct
13. *(he, she)* seizes

Down

1. faith
2. returning
3. terms
4. accountants
5. thresholds, doorsteps
7. chin
8. *(I)* would be
11. *(he, she)* laughs

accountant = comptable (f)

threshold = seuil (m)

No. 73

Across

1. pleasure
5. dared
7. *(and)* then
9. *(to)* him/her
10. floor
11. *(he, she)* leaves *(behind)* *(I)* leave *(behind)*
13. arabs
15. your
17. *(they)* have
18. more
20. above, on top
21. furthermore, besides, on top of that *(2,5)*

Down

1. rained pleased
2. years
3. to greet
4. kings
6. churches
7. pilots
8. here
12. to jump, leap
14. ball
16. compass point
18. footstep not
19. a, an *(fem)*

No. 74

Across

1. awful, loathsome
7. fairy
8. this
9. tail
10. level
13. to pour
15. between
16. to name
18. sight, view
19. syringe

Down

2. goose
3. queen
4. small boat
5. effects
6. to live, stay, remain
8. preserved
11. window panes
12. the future
14. novel
17. water

No. 75

Across

1. bowls
3. positioned
6. elsewhere
9. they
10. shout, scream
11. file *(tool)*
13. to deny
14. you
16. early
17. *(he, she)* will arrive
20. monkey
21. *(they)* do, make

Down

1. white
2. salt
3. not much, little
4. plate
5. summers
7. distant
8. she
12. *(I)* will go
15. *(he, she)* would go
16. very
18. street, road
19. lively; vivid

positioned = placé

file = lime (f)

No. 76

Across

1. marked
4. these
6. to interest
7. brush
   paintbrush
9. error
   mistake
10. *(horse drawn)* carts
12. *(he, she)* is
    east
13. grape

Down

1. me
2. *(he, she)* was finding *(again)*
3. to raise, bring up
4. caps
5. to go out, exit
7. mouth
8. to tighten; to shake *(hands)*
11. his, her, its
    sound

cap = casquette (f)

No. 77

Across

1. bus stop *(5,2,3)*
6. year
7. court
8. to tighten
   tender *(soft, delicate)*
10. *(you/tu)* offer
13. night
14. so, such, thereby, thus
15. actually, really

Down

1. to give up
   to abandon, forsake
2. row
3. thirty
4. fair, fair-haired
5. on the brink *(of)*, on the verge *(of)* *(3,2,5)*
9. room, space
11. to make
    to do
12. angel

court = cour (m)

row = rang (m)

1 d	i	2 s	■	3 b	a	l	4 l	o	5 n
u	■	a	■	e	■	■	a	■	o
6 c	h	i	r	u	r	g	i	e	n
o	■	s	■	r	■	■	s	■	■
u	■	i	■	7 r	8 a	i	s	o	9 n
10 p	a	s	s	e	r	■	a	■	a
■	■	s	■	■	d	■	i	■	î
11 c	h	a	n	g	e	m	e	n	t
a	■	n	■	■	u	■	n	■	r
12 r	e	t	o	u	r	■	13 t	u	e

Across

1. *(you/tu)* say
   (I) say
3. balloon
   football, soccer ball
6. surgeon
7. reason
10. to cross, go through, get over
    to pass
11. change
12. return
13. *(I)* kill

Down

1. so, as a result *(2,4)*
2. seizing
3. butter
4. *(they)* were leaving *(behind)*
5. no
8. ardour
9. to be born
11. because, since

Surgeon = chirurgien (m) | So = du coup

No. 79

Across

1. dice
3. each
6. *(they)* would be able to
7. *(you/tu)* used to know *(I)* used to know
10. schools
11. *(they)* were missing
12. *(they)* will be
13. certain, sure

Down

1. deposited
2. to suspect
3. cherry
4. knights
5. clear, distinct
8. assault
9. to smell to feel
11. put, placed

dice = dé (m)

to suspect = soupçonner

No. 80

1 R	2 A	P	3 P	O	4 R	T	5 S	■	6 J
■	I	■	A	■	E	■	7 U	N	E
8 P	R	9 I	S	■	10 I	C	I	■	U
R	■	R	■	■	N	■	11 T	O	N
12 O	R	A	N	13 G	E	■	■	■	E
B	■	■	■	14 E	S	S	15 A	I	S
16 L	I	17 S	■	N	■	■	M	■	S
È	■	18 O	N	T	■	19 R	I	20 V	E
21 M	A	I	■	I	■	O	■	I	■
E	■	22 F	A	L	A	I	S	E	S

Across

1. reports
7. a, an *(fem)*
8. taken
10. here
11. your
12. a citrus fruit
14. tests, trials
16. *(I)* read
18. *(they)* have
19. bank *(of a river)*
21. month of the year
22. cliffs

Down

2. appearance, look
3. footstep
   not
4. queens
5. *(he, she)* follows
6. youth, adolescence
8. problem
9. *(he, she)* will go
13. kind, nice
15. friend
17. thirst
19. king
20. life

cliff = falaise (f.)

1 D	O	2 U	B	L	3 E	■	4 M	E	5 R
O	■	N	■	■	X	■	É	■	A
6 N	A	I	S	S	A	N	C	E	S
■	■	V	■	■	M	■	A	■	E
7 P	L	E	U	8 R	E	■	N	■	U
E	■	R	■	9 E	N	T	I	E	R
N	■	S	■	V	■	■	C	■	■
10 C	H	I	R	U	R	G	I	É	11 S
H	■	T	■	E	■	■	E	■	U
12 É	T	É	■	13 S	O	N	N	E	R

Across

1. dual, twofold
4. sea
6. births
7. *(I)* cry
9. whole, entire
10. surgeries
12. season of the year
13. to ring, to sound

Down

1. gift
2. college, university
3. examination
4. mechanic
5. razor
7. leaning
8. reviews
11. above, on top

dual = double

gift = don (m)

leaning = penché

No. 82

Across

1. product
5. water
6. they
7. sword
10. case, instance
11. acquired
13. one day, at some time, eventually *(2,4)*
15. gay
 cheerful
16. below, under
19. wall
20. goose
21. churches

Down

1. *(and)* then
2. bird
3. used
 worn *(out, down)*
4. killed
5. in progress, underway *(2,5)*
8. not much, little
9. subsequently, next
12. offences against the law
14. game
15. big, thick, fat
17. dared
18. salt

No. 83

■	■	1 C	O	2 M	P	3 T	E	4 S	■
5 C	R	U	■	U	■	I	■	O	■
É	■	I	■	6 S	E	R	O	N	7 S
8 L	I	V	R	É	■	E	■	■	O
È	■	R	■	9 E	10 R	R	11 E	U	R
12 B	L	E	13 S	S	É	■	F	■	T
R	■	■	H	■	14 S	U	F	F	I
15 E	16 N	V	O	I	E	■	E	■	E
■	O	■	R	■	A	■	17 T	A	S
■	18 M	O	T	E	U	R	S	■	■

Across

1. accounts
5. believed
raw
6. *(we)* will be
8. delivered
9. error
mistake
12. injured
14. sufficed
15. *(I)* send
17. heap, pile
18. motors

Down

1. copper
2. museums
3. to draw, drag, pull
to shoot
4. his, her, its
sound
5. famous, renowned
7. exits
10. net, network
11. effects
13. shorts
16. name

deliver = livrer

copper = cuivre (m)

famous = célèbre

No. 84

Across

2. nobility
6. rained
 pleased
7. fixed
9. rule
10. atrocious
13. obscure, dim
15. finally, in the end
16. witness
18. street, road
19. judgment

Down

1. *(he, she)* glimpses, catches sight of
2. clouds
3. office
4. hell
5. six
8. to sneeze
11. thirty
12. offered
14. thing
17. elected

atrocious = atroce
witness = témoin (m)

sneeze = éternuer

No. 85

Across

1. glass
4. baby
6. to tie, fasten
9. floor
10. *(I)* will go
12. *(he, she)* drank
    aim, goal
13. tired, weary
14. this
15. bed
17. as, because, for, since *(5,3)*
20. black
21. ideas

Down

1. views
2. to achieve, fulfill
3. *(he, she)* is
   east
4. beak
5. *(he, she)* writes
7. a *(female)* friend
8. skill
11. act
    action
13. rabbit
16. very
18. because, since
19. who

No. 86

■	1 D	E	2 L	I	3 C	A	4 T	■	■
■	U	■	I	■	H	■	5 O	U	6 I
7 P	R	È	S	D	E	■	U	■	N
A	■	■	T	■	8 M	A	R	I	S
9 S	A	10 M	E	11 D	I	■	N	■	P
S	■	I	■	12 E	N	13 N	E	M	I
14 A	B	R	I	S	■	A	■	■	R
I	■	O	■	15 S	É	P	A	16 R	É
17 T	O	I	■	U	■	P	■	I	■
■	■	18 R	E	S	P	E	C	T	■

Across

1. delicate
5. yes
7. next to *(4,2)*
8. husbands
9. day of the week
12. foe
14. shelters
15. separated
17. you
18. consideration

Down

1. hard
2. list
3. path, way
4. *(I)* turn
6. inspired
7. *(he, she)* was passing
10. mirror
11. on top of
13. tablecloth
16. *(he, she)* laughs

Shelter = abri (m)

No. 87

1 S	U	2 D	■	3 V	O	Y	4 A	I	5 S
A	■	É	■	E	■	■	S	■	Û
6 I	N	T	É	R	E	S	S	E	R
S	■	E	■	S	■	■	U	■	■
O	■	R	■	7 E	8 S	P	R	I	9 T
10 N	O	M	B	R	E	■	E	■	A
■	■	I	■	■	R	■	M	■	N
11 M	A	N	Q	U	A	I	E	N	T
O	■	E	■	■	I	■	N	■	Ô
12 T	I	R	A	I	T	■	13 T	Ô	T

Across

1. compass point
3. *(I)* was seeing *(you/tu)* were seeing
6. to interest
7. spirit; mind
10. amount, number
11. *(they)* were missing
12. *(he, she)* was shooting, drawing
13. early

Down

1. season
2. to determine, establish
3. to pour
4. assuredly, certainly
5. certain, sure
8. *(he, she)* would
9. sometimes
11. word

No. 88

Across

1. product
5. fire
6. *(he, she)* will go
7. she
10. years
11. left, left-hand
13. middle
    setting, environment
15. lively; vivid
16. *(he, she)* knows
19. friend
20. *(he, she)* says
21. playhouse

Down

1. *(and)* then
2. a citrus fruit
3. a, an *(fem)*
4. such
5. flames
8. lake
9. indeed, actually *(2,5)*
12. *(he, she)* would have
14. *(to)* him/her
15. empty
17. painting, theatre, music etc
18. tea

No. 89

Across

1. pumpkin
6. brought
7. overly, too, too much
8. error
   mistake
10. *(I)* hope
13. roof
14. trunk
15. towels

Down

1. *(horse drawn)* carts
2. to kill
3. to operate
4. wide, broad
5. hopes, expectations
9. *(I)* go back in
   (he, she) goes back in
11. to pray
12. lot, fate
    (he, she) goes out

expectation = espérance (f)

No. 90

1 E	■	■	2 S	3 E	R	4 V	A	5 I	T
6 M	E	7 R	■	N	■	I	■	L	■
P	■	8 E	W	F	A	N	9 T	S	■
10 O	N	T	■	A	■	■	R	■	11 A
R	■	E	■	12 C	13 A	P	O	T	S
14 T	E	N	T	E	R	■	U	■	S
É	■	I	■	■	R	■	15 V	I	E
■	16 O	R	17 I	G	I	N	E	■	O
■	S	■	C	■	V	■	18 R	O	I
19 M	E	R	I	T	E	R	■	■	R

Across

2. *(he, she)* was serving
6. sea
8. children
10. *(they)* have
12. hoods
14. to tempt
    to try
15. life
16. starting point
18. king
19. to deserve, merit

Down

1. taken away
3. opposite *(2,4)*
4. wine
5. they
7. to hold back, detain
9. to find
11. to sit down
13. *(I)* get to, reach
16. dared
17. here

taken away = emporté

1 P	■	2 A	I	3 G	U	4 I	L	5 L	E
6 É	M	U	■	Â	■	R	■	I	■
R	■	R	■	7 T	R	A	I	T	8 S
9 I	M	A	G	E	■	I	■	■	E
O	■	I	■	10 A	11 C	T	12 E	U	R
13 D	È	S	14 Q	U	E	■	F	■	A
E	■	■	U	■	15 S	U	F	F	I
16 S	17 E	R	A	I	S	■	E	■	E
■	A	■	R	■	E	■	18 T	O	N
19 G	U	I	T	A	R	E	S	■	T

Across

2. needle
6. *(emotionally)* touched, moved
7. features
9. picture
10. actor
13. once, as soon as *(3,3)*
15. sufficed
16. *(I)* would be
18. your
19. guitars

Down

1. periods
2. *(I)* would have
3. cake
4. *(he, she)* would go
5. bed
8. *(they)* would be
11. to cease
12. effects
14. fourth, quarter
17. water

needle = aiguille (f)

No. 92

1 A	U	2 F	A	I	3 T	■	4 S	O	5 L
I	■	I	■	■	U	■	E	■	I
6 R	E	N	C	O	N	T	R	E	S
■	■	A	■	■	N	■	V	■	A
7 V	A	L	L	8 E	E	■	I	■	I
O	■	E	■	9 P	L	U	T	Ô	T
L	■	M	■	I	■	■	E	■	■
10 C	H	E	R	C	H	E	U	R	11 S
A	■	N	■	E	■	■	R	■	U
12 N	E	T	■	13 S	A	I	S	I	R

Across

1. by the way, in fact *(2,4)*
4. floor
6. meetings
   (you/tu) meet
7. valley
9. rather
10. researchers
    searchers
12. clear, distinct
13. to seize, grab

Down

1. appearance, look
2. finally
3. an underground passage
4. servants
5. *(he, she)* was reading
7. volcano
8. spices
11. above, on top

researcher = chercheur (m)

No. 93

Across

2. dragged away, pulled along
   exercised, coached
6. to the *(plural)*
7. *(I)* lead
9. lost
10. mother or father
13. to stay
    to remain
15. morning
16. discarded, removed, separated
18. wall
19. pianist

Down

1. reported
2. on purpose
3. troop
4. to love, like
5. no
8. to hear
11. armies
12. respect, regard
14. dictator, despot
17. shout, scream

No. 94

Across

1. season of the year
3. *(you/tu)* close
6. flood
7. lettuce
10. *(we)* are
11. make-up
12. glows
13. you

Down

1. sinks
2. economic
3. faithful
4. at present, now
5. his, her, its sound
8. asylums
9. foe
11. bad, wrong pain

flood = inondation (f)

sink = évier

faithful = fidèle

No. 95

Across

1. strollers
6. night
7. to come
8. warned, averted
10. *(he, she)* goes back in *(I)* go back in
13. quays, docks
14. state, condition
15. interviews

Down

1. while, as *(7,3)*
2. useful
3. *(I)* send
4. held
5. towels
9. sad
11. title
12. *(it)* is worth

Stroller = poussette (f)

to warn = avertir

No. 96

1 M	O	T	2 S	■	3 C	L	4 E	F	5 S
A	■	■	Û	■	R	■	X	■	O
6 R	E	7 T	R	8 O	U	V	E	■	N
I	■	O	■	N	■	■	9 M	E	T
10 N	O	M	■	11 D	12 R	A	P	■	■
■	■	13 B	L	E	U	■	14 L	I	15 S
16 F	É	E	■	■	D	■	E	■	E
O	■	17 A	D	18 R	E	19 S	S	E	R
N	■	U	■	U	■	U	■	■	A
20 T	E	X	T	E	■	21 B	O	I	S

Across

1. words
3. keys
6. *(he, she)* finds *(again)*
   (I) find *(again)*
9. *(he, she)* puts
10. name
11. sheet
13. blue
14. *(I)* read
16. fairy
17. to direct, address
20. piece of writing
21. *(I)* must

Down

1. sailor
2. certain, sure
3. believed
   raw
4. examples
5. *(they)* are
7. tombs
8. wave
12. rough, harsh
15. *(you)* will be
16. *(they)* do, make
18. street, road
19. compass point

✓

No. 97

1 M	A	2 I	■	3 G	O	U	4 T	T	5 E
A	■	N	■	L	■	■	R	■	S
6 R	E	T	R	O	U	V	A	I	T
Q	■	E	■	I	■	■	V	■	■
U	■	R	■	7 R	8 O	M	A	N	9 S
10 E	L	E	V	E	R	■	I	■	A
■	■	S	■	■	D	■	L	■	I
11 C	A	S	S	E	R	O	L	E	S
O	■	E	■	■	Ê	■	E	■	I
12 L	A	R	M	E	S	■	13 R	I	T

Across

1. month of the year
3. drop
6. *(he, she)* was finding *(again)*
7. novels
10. to raise, bring up
11. saucepans
12. teardrops
13. *(he, she)* laughs

Down

1. marked
2. to interest
3. glory
4. to work
5. *(he, she)* is east
8. orders
9. *(he, she)* seizes
11. collar

drop = goutte (f)

teardrop = larme (f)

No. 98

Across

1. *(he, she)* goes down
5. yes
7. prize
   price
9. not much, little
10. elected
11. to kiss
13. filled
15. *(he, she)* will go
17. life
18. *(I)* pray
20. king
21. surprised

Down

1. hard
2. six
3. *(I)* hope
4. gifted
6. unused; useless
7. to publish
8. here
12. error
    mistake
14. pure
16. opinion
    advice
18. by, by means of
    at the rate of, per
19. they

fill = remplacer

Across

1. agreeable, nice
7. my
8. god, deity
9. chamber, room, ward
10. although, even though *(4,2)*
    even if *(4,2)*
13. old, former, ex-
15. conceived
16. tree trunks
18. law
19. terrors

Down

2. cheerful
   gay
3. study
4. basin
5. job, employment
6. antennas
8. home, residence
11. *(he, she)* was leading
12. to jump, leap
14. thing
17. because, since

basin = bassin (m)

antenna = antenne (f)

No. 100

Across

1. planted
4. case, instance
6. shampoo
7. present, gift
9. took back; resumed
10. toothpaste
12. above, on top
13. extensive; widespread

Down

1. footstep
   not
2. to give up
   to abandon, forsake
3. epoch
4. surgeon
5. marks, symbols
7. ropes
8. arrived
11. water

took back = reprendre

toothpaste = dentifrice (f)

extensive = étendu

No. 101

■	■	1 s	é	2 j	o	3 u	r	4 s	■
5 v	u	e	■	o	■	n	■	e	■
e	■	6 p	l	u	■	7 e	8 l	l	9 e
10 n	e	t	■	e	■	■	i	■	n
t	■	■	■	11 n	12 a	î	t	r	e
13 r	é	14 c	i	t	s	■	■	■	f
e	■	r	■	■	s	■	15 v	i	f
16 s	17 a	i	18 t	■	19 a	m	i	■	e
■	r	■	h	■	u	■	20 d	i	t
■	21 t	h	é	a	t	r	e	■	■

Across

1. stays, visits
5. sight, view
6. rained
   pleased
7. she
10. clear, distinct
11. to be born
13. stories, tales
15. lively; vivid
16. *(he, she)* knows
19. friend
20. *(he, she)* says
21. playhouse

Down

1. seven
2. *(they)* play
3. a, an *(fem)*
4. salt
5. bellies
8. bed
9. indeed, actually *(2,5)*
12. assault
14. shout, scream
15. empty
17. painting, theatre, music etc
18. tea

story = récit (m)

belly = ventre (m)

Across

1. juice
3. *(he, she)* will be able
6. descendant, offspring, successor
7. pens
10. entrance
11. *(they)* were leaving *(behind)*
12. extinguished, out extinct
13. *(I)* kill

Down

1. until, up to
2. secretary
3. pressed, squeezed
4. actually, really
5. appearance, look
8. *(he, she)* was holding
9. exit, way out
11. linked

No. 103

Across

1. stomach
5. tired, weary
6. lettuce
9. wall
10. drunk, drunken, intoxicated
12. *(he, she)* puts
13. early
14. act
    action
15. no
16. submitted
20. believed
    raw
21. strange

Down

1. spirit; mind
2. such
3. me
4. neck
5. confines, borders
7. with
8. heard; understood
11. thrilled, delighted
12. threat
17. dared
18. sea
19. his, her, its
    sound

No. 104

Across

1. properties
6. nerves
7. to flee, run away
8. *(he, she)* leaves *(behind)* *(I)* leave *(behind)*
10. one day, at some time, eventually *(2,4)*
13. wolf
14. broom
15. seizing

Down

1. slippers
2. bear
3. resolved
4. turns towers
5. on the brink *(of)*, on the verge *(of)* *(3,2,5)*
9. arabs
11. day of the week
12. there are, there is *(2,1,1)*

No. 105

Across

1. by, by means of
   at the rate of, per
3. ill, sick
6. *(they)* were missing
7. worries
10. to think about, ponder
11. character *(in a play, program, film)*
12. risk
13. you

Down

1. apples
2. meetings
   (you/tu) meet
3. froth, foam; moss
4. *(he, she)* was glimpsing
5. *(he, she)* is
   east
8. a citrus fruit
9. day of the week
11. pure

No. 106

Across

1. attracted
4. bad, wrong
   pain
6. to suspect
7. present, gift
9. *(I)* would be
10. teacher
12. compass point
13. sometimes

Down

1. years
2. above all, especially, primarily *(4,1,5)*
3. epoch
4. *(they)* were showing
5. teardrops
7. cuts
8. appearance, look
   facet, angle
11. *(he, she)* laughs

No. 107

1 P	2 R	É	3 F	E	4 R	I	■	■	5 P
■	O	■	E	■	E	■	6 L	U	I
■	7 I	8 N	U	T	I	L	E	■	E
9 G	■	A	■	■	N	■	10 C	A	R
11 A	R	R	I	12 V	E	■	T	■	R
R	■	I	■	13 A	S	S	U	R	E
14 D	O	N	■	L	■	■	R	■	S
A	■	15 E	N	L	E	16 V	E	17 R	■
18 I	L	S	■	É	■	I	■	U	■
T	■	■	19 D	E	R	N	I	E	R

Across

1. favorite, preferred
6. *(to)* him/her
7. unused; useless
10. because, since
11. *(I)* get to, reach
13. *(I)* make sure
14. gift
15. to remove, take off
18. they
19. last, latest

Down

2. king
3. fire
4. queens
5. stones
6. reading
8. nostrils
9. *(he, she)* kept
12. valley
16. wine
17. street, road

keep = garder

No. 108

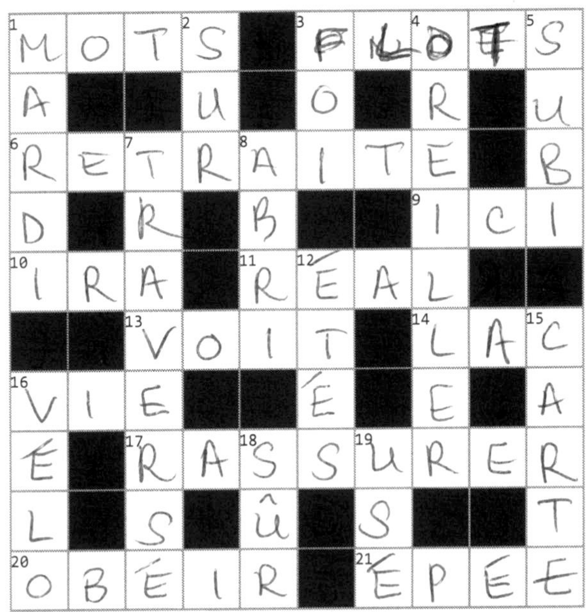

Across

1. words
3. waves, floods
6. retreat, retirement
9. here
10. *(he, she)* will go
11. actual
13. *(he, she)* sees
14. lake
16. life
17. to reassure
20. to obey
21. sword

Down

1. day of the week
2. above, on top
3. faith
4. pillow
5. suffered, endured
7. crossed
8. shelter
12. summers
15. card
    map
16. bicycle
18. certain, sure
19. used
    worn *(out, down)*

waves = flots (m.)

retreat = retraite (f)

pillow = oreiller (m)

Suffer = Subir

Shelter = abri (m)

No. 109

Across

1. *(he, she)* forces
   (I) force
4. son
6. *(it)* would be necessary, would have to
9. salt
10. equal, even, level
12. tea
13. dry
14. railway station
15. name
17. distant
20. roof
21. remainder

Down

1. fairies
2. pondered, reflected
3. water
4. iron
5. situated
7. some *(2,2)*
   of the *(2,2)*
8. antennas
11. *(he, she)* acts
13. hello; goodbye
16. even
    same
18. clear, distinct
19. appearance, look

No. 110

1 P	H	2 A	R	3 M	A	C	4 I	E	5 N
A	■	B	■	E	■	■	R	■	O
6 S	U	B	I	T	■	7 P	A	R	U
S	■	E	■	T	■	■	I	■	R
E	■	■	■	8 R	9 E	S	T	E	R
10 P	A	11 T	T	E	S	■	■	■	I
O	■	I	■	■	P	■	12 P	■	T
13 R	I	R	E	■	14 A	D	I	E	U
T	■	E	■	■	C	■	E	■	R
15 S	O	R	P	R	E	N	D	R	E

Across

1. pharmacist
6. abrupt, sudden
7. appeared
8. to stay
   to remain
10. paws
13. to laugh
14. farewell
15. to surprise

Down

1. passports
2. abbot
3. to put
4. *(he, she)* would go
5. food
9. room, space
11. to draw, drag, pull
    to shoot
12. foot

No. 111

Across

2. pressure
6. sight, view
7. hunger
9. tablecloth
10. home
13. the future
15. twelve
16. *(I)* turn
18. law
19. springs *(coiled devices)*

Down

1. *(it)* was advancing
2. people *(of a nation)*
3. foe
4. sufficed
5. yes
8. *(he, she)* was eating
11. ardour
12. thresholds, doorsteps
14. nerves
17. goose

■	■	1 m	e	2 d	e	3 c	i	4 n	■
5 p	l	u	■	i	■	r	■	o	■
i	■	s	■	6 t	7 o	u	r	n	8 é
9 l	i	é	■	■	s	■	■	■	g
o	■	10 e	l	11 l	e	■	12 t	e	l
13 t	a	s	■	14 i	r	a	i	■	i
e	■	■	■	m	■	■	15 m	i	s
16 s	17 o	m	18 m	e	19 s	■	i	■	e
■	s	■	e	■	o	■	20 d	i	s
■	21 é	t	r	a	n	g	e	■	■

Across

1. medical doctor
5. pleased
rained
6. turned
9. linked
10. she
12. such
13. heap, pile
14. *(I)* will go
15. put, placed
16. *(we)* are
20. dice
21. strange

Down

1. museums
2. *(he, she)* says
3. believed
raw
4. no
5. pilots
7. to dare
8. churches
11. file *(tool)*
12. shy
17. dared
18. sea
19. his, her, its
sound

No. 113

1 a	n	2 s	■	3 b	a	n	4 a	n	5 e
p	■	o	■	u	■	■	p	■	s
6 p	o	u	v	r	a	i	e	n	t
e	■	p	■	e	■	■	r	■	■
l	■	ç	■	7 a	8 v	o	c	a	9 t
10 e	p	o	q	u	e	■	e	■	a
■	■	n	■	■	r	■	v	■	n
11 c	o	n	c	e	r	n	a	n	t
o	■	e	■	■	e	■	i	■	ô
12 l	a	r	m	e	s	■	13 t	ô	t

Across

1. years
3. banana
6. *(they)* would be able to
7. lawyer
10. epoch
11. concerning, regarding
12. teardrops
13. early

Down

1. called
2. to suspect
3. office
4. *(he, she)* was glimpsing
5. *(he, she)* is east
8. glasses
9. sometimes
11. collar

suspect = soupçonner

glasses = verre (m)

No. 114

Across

2. stormy
6. hard
8. *(I)* express
   (he, she) expresses
10. *(they)* have
12. to give
14. to try
    to tempt
15. you
16. fear
18. floor
19. to arrive
    to happen

Down

1. on the right *(1,6)*
3. fast
4. gay
   cheerful
5. a, an *(fem)*
7. to hold back, detain
9. divisions of time
11. ear
13. a citrus fruit
16. because, since
17. friend

No. 115

Across

1. by, by means of at the rate of, per
3. to admit
6. necessary, needful
7. rejected
10. queens
11. generation
12. lists
13. *(emotionally)* touched, moved

Down

1. to think
2. containers
3. *(I)* make sure
4. college, university
5. street, road
8. tests, trials
9. extensive; widespread
11. frost

admit = avouer

rejected = rejeté

container = récipient (m)

extensive = étendu

No. 116

1 R	Ê	2 V	E	3 R	■	4 J	U	G	5 É
E	■	É	■	O	■	U	■	■	C
A	■	6 R	U	I	7 S	S	8 E	A	U
9 L	U	I	■	■	E	■	N	■	M
■	■	10 F	E	11 R	A	■	12 F	É	E
13 F	O	I	■	14 A	U	R	A	■	■
Â	■	E	■	C	■	■	15 C	E	16 S
17 C	E	R	18 V	E	19 L	L	E	■	U
H	■	■	I	■	A	■	D	■	I
20 É	T	A	T	■	21 C	L	E	F	S

Across

1. to dream
4. judged
6. brook, creek, stream
9. *(to)* him/her
10. *(he, she)* will do
12. fairy
13. faith
14. *(he, she)* will have
15. these
17. brain
20. state, condition
21. keys

Down

1. actual
2. to verify
3. king
4. juice
5. foam
7. bucket
8. opposite *(2,4,2)*
11. ethnic class of people
13. angry
16. *(I)* am
18. *(he, she)* lives
19. lake

brook = ruisseau (m)

foam = écume (f)
bucket = seau (m)
angry = fâché

No. 117

1 C	O	2 N	T	3 I	N	U	4 A	N	5 T
A	■	O	■	M	■	■	U	■	E
6 S	E	R	A	I	■	7 Ô	T	E	R
S	■	D	■	T	■	■	E	■	R
E	■	■	■	8 E	9 M	P	L	O	I
10 R	O	11 M	P	R	E	■	■	■	T
O	■	E	■	■	T	■	12 T	■	O
13 L	O	N	G	■	14 T	R	A	H	I
E	■	E	■	■	R	■	R	■	R
15 S	O	R	P	R	E	N	D	R	E

Across

1. continuing
6. *(I)* will be
7. to take away, remove
8. job, employment
10. to break
13. lengthy
14. betrayed
15. to surprise

Down

1. saucepans
2. compass point
3. to mimic, copy
4. altar
5. territory, turf
9. to put
11. to lead, to take
12. late

remove = ôter

altar = autel (m)

No. 118

Across

1. pocket
4. sounds
6. *(he, she)* would be able to
9. above, on top
10. drunk, drunken, intoxicated
12. tea
13. beak
14. angel
15. nose
17. immediately
20. heaven, sky
21. our

Down

1. folds
2. whims
3. water
4. certain, sure
5. situated
7. nothing
8. attack, assault
11. thrilled, delighted
13. white
16. ardour, fervour, zeal
18. salt
19. your

beak = bec ( )

fold = pli ( )

attack = attentat ( )

zeal = zèle ( )

No. 119

Across

1. to convince
6. hands
7. all
   everything
8. to be born
10. shot down, cut down
13. laws
14. driveway
15. servants

Down

1. accountants
2. nut
3. not there
4. *(he, she)* believes
5. interviews
9. *(he, she)* would have
11. steel
12. blue

Shotdown = abatir

acc = comptable (m)

not there = absent

Steel = acier (m)

No. 120

Across

1. properties
6. nerves
7. for, to
8. *(he, she)* leaves *(behind)* *(I)* leave *(behind)*
10. one day, at some time, eventually *(2,4)*
13. wolf
14. broom
15. seizing

Down

1. slippers
2. bear
3. resolved
4. holes
5. on the brink *(of)*, on the verge *(of)* *(3,2,5)*
9. arabs
11. day of the week
12. there are, there is *(2,1,1)*

property = propriété (f)

broom = balai (m)

hole = trou (m)

No. 121

■	■	1 F	A	2 L	A	3 I	S	4 E	■
5 M	A	I	■	E	■	R	■	S	■
É	■	G	■	6 T	R	A	I	T	7 S
8 C	O	U	R	T	■	I	■	■	O
H	■	R	■	9 R	10 E	T	11 E	N	U
12 A	M	E	13 N	E	R	■	N	■	V
N	■	■	U	■	14 R	I	C	H	E
15 T	16 I	M	I	D	E	■	O	■	N
■	R	■	T	■	U	■	17 R	I	T
■	18 A	B	S	U	R	D	E	■	■

Across

1. cliff
5. month of the year
6. features
8. short
9. retained
12. to bring
14. rich
15. shy
17. *(he, she)* laughs
18. crazy

Down

1. face
2. letter
3. *(he, she)* would go
4. *(he, she)* is
east
5. evil, wicked
7. often
10. error
mistake
11. again
still, yet
13. nights
16. *(he, she)* will go

cliff = falaise
short = court

evil = méchant

face = figure

No. 122

Across

2. condemned
6. sight, view
7. name
8. blood
11. clear, distinct
12. to stay
to remain
14. old, former, ex-
16. wine
17. wrong; fault
20. friend
21. you
22. amount of space between two points

Down

1. *(it)* was advancing
2. hundred
3. amount, number
4. years
5. no
9. painting, theatre, music etc
10. to guarantee
13. in vain, to no avail, uselessly *(2,4)*
15. because, since
16. quick, fast
18. yes
19. early

condemn = condamner

No. 123

Across

1. deposited
4. goose
6. births
7. not bad *(3,3)*
9. *(I)* would be
10. easily, readily
12. put, placed
13. exit, way out

Down

1. gift
2. powers
3. shoulder
4. *(they)* were occupying
5. tests, trials
7. perfume
8. asylums
11. *(I)* kill

No. 124

1 E	■	2 C	E	3 I	N	4 T	U	5 R	E
6 S	O	L	■	L	■	E	■	U	■
C	■	O	■	7 S	8 A	L	L	E	9 S
10 L	A	C	■	■	C	■	■	■	E
A	■	11 H	U	12 I	T	■	13 S	O	N
14 V	I	E	■	15 D	E	L	A	■	T
E	■	■	■	É	■	■	16 M	O	I
17 S	18 O	M	19 M	E	20 S	■	E	■	E
■	S	■	A	■	E	■	21 D	U	R
22 R	É	F	L	E	C	H	I	■	S

Across

2. belt
6. floor
7. rooms
10. lake
11. eight
13. his, her, its
sound
14. life
15. some *(2,2)*
of the *(2,2)*
16. me
17. *(we)* are
21. hard
22. pondered, reflected

Down

1. slaves
2. bell
3. they
4. such
5. street, road
8. act
action
9. trails, paths
12. notion
13. day of the week
18. dared
19. bad, wrong
pain
20. dry

Slave = esclave (M)

trail = sentier (m)

No. 125

1 P	R	2 É	S	E	3 N	T	4 E	N	5 T
H		V			A		L		E
6 A	G	I	T		7 V	O	L	E	R
R		E			I		E		R
8 M	A	R	I	9 E	R				I
A				10 F	E	R	11 A	I	T
C		12 B		F			U		O
13 I	M	A	G	E		14 I	R	A	I
E		N		T			A		R
15 N	É	C	E	S	S	A	I	R	E

Across

1. *(they)* present
6. *(he, she)* acts
7. to fly
   to steal
8. to marry
10. *(he, she)* would do, make
13. picture
14. *(I)* will go
15. necessary, needful

Down

1. pharmacist
2. sink, basin
3. ship
4. she
5. territory, turf
9. effects
11. *(I)* will have
12. bench

act = agir | sink = évier (m)

Solutions

No. 1

a		m	e	r	c	r	e	d	i
f	é	e		â		i		u	
f		t	ô	t		t	i	r	e
i	l	s		e			r		n
r				a	s	s	a	u	t
m	a	n	q	u	e				e
e		o			r		s	o	n
r	e	n	d		o	i	e		d
	a		o		n		r	u	e
a	u	s	s	i	t	ô	t		z

No. 2

v	o	u	d	r	a		f	i	l
i		n			v		a		i
n	a	i	s	s	a	n	c	e	s
		v			l		i		a
p	i	e	r	r	e		l		i
o		r		a	r	g	e	n	t
u		s		i			m		
l	a	i	s	s	a	i	e	n	t
e		t		i			n		u
t	h	é		n	a	î	t	r	e

No. 3

		q	u	e	l	q	u	e	
f	e	u		m		u		s	
r		i		p	l	a	n	t	e
a	u	t	e	l		i			r
p		t		o	b	s	c	u	r
p	o	é	s	i	e		a		e
e			e		u	n	p	e	u
r	é	g	n	e	r		o		r
	l		t		r		t	a	s
	u	n	i	v	e	r	s		

No. 4

		a	r	r	a	c	h	é	
s	u	r		é		e		m	
o		m	i	s		s	œ	u	r
u	n	e		e			i		i
r				a	s	i	l	e	s
c	h	a	q	u	e				q
i		m			m		p	l	u
l	o	i	n		b	a	l		e
	n		o		l		a	i	r
	t	o	m	b	e	n	t		

No. 5

s	h	a	m	p	o	o	i	n	g
u		c		a			r		é
b	a	t	t	u		m	a	i	n
i		e		v			i		é
t				r	e	s	t	e	r
e	x	a	m	e	n				a
m		l			f		p		t
e	l	l	e		a	u	r	a	i
n		é			c		ê		o
t	r	e	n	t	e	e	t	u	n

No. 6

p	a	r		s	o	m	m	e	t
o		é		e			a		o
m	é	c	a	n	i	c	i	e	n
m		o		t			n		
e		m		i	m	i	t	e	r
s	é	p	a	r	é		e		e
		e			p		n		n
c	o	n	c	e	r	n	a	n	t
o		s			i		n		r
l	u	e	u	r	s		t	u	é

Solutions

No. 7

s	a	i	s		s	e	l	o	n
e			o		e		a		o
r	é	f	l	é	c	h	i		i
a		o		t			s	i	x
s	û	r		a	v	i	s		
		m	o	t	o		a	r	t
c	r	u			i		n		a
e		l	u	n	e	t	t	e	s
l		e		e		e			s
a	s	s	e	z		l	è	v	e

No. 8

p	r	o	f	o	n	d			r
	u		i		a		f	o	i
	e	n	l	e	v	e	r		v
à		a			i		o	u	i
s	o	r	t	i	r		t		è
a		i		m	e	n	t	i	r
v	i	n		p			e		e
o		e	n	o	u	t	r	e	
i	l	s		s		o		a	
r			s	é	r	i	e	u	x

No. 9

l	i	s	a	i	t		c	a	s
a		i			r		a		e
c	o	m	p	t	e	r	s	u	r
		p			n		s		i
s	o	l	d	a	t		e		e
o		e		v	e	r	r	e	z
n		m		i			o		
g	r	e	n	o	u	i	l	l	e
e		n		n			e		s
r	i	t		s	a	i	s	i	t

No. 10

e	n	c	h	a	n	t	é		d
	o		a		a		v	i	e
a	m	e	r		î		i		m
c			d		t	i	t	r	e
c	a	s	i	e	r		e		u
o		e		s	e	r	r	e	r
m	a	r	i	s		i			e
p		v		a	r	d	e	u	r
l	o	i		i		e		n	
i		r	é	s	i	s	t	e	r

No. 11

l	a	r	m	e	s		d	u	r
u			e		o		i		e
i	n	s	t	a	n	t	s		s
		o		i			t	ô	t
p	l	u		s	o	i	r		e
r		r	i	e	n		a	n	s
i	c	i			z		i		
s		a	c	c	e	p	t	e	r
o		n		e		e			o
n	e	t		s	a	u	r	a	i

No. 12

		d	i	s	c	r	e	t	
s	u	r		a		e		u	
o		o		m	o	n	t	e	r
r	e	i	n	e		d			i
t		t		d	e	s	s	u	s
a	v	e	n	i	r		i		q
i			u		r	o	m	p	u
t	i	m	i	d	e		p		e
	r		t		u		l	a	s
	a	b	s	u	r	d	e		

Solutions

No. 13

a	r	r	ê	t	d	e	b	u	s
b	■	o	■	e	■	■	l	■	u
a	u	s	s	i	■	j	o	u	r
n	■	e	■	n	■	■	n	■	l
d	■	■	■	t	e	n	d	r	e
o	f	f	r	e	s	■	■	■	p
n	■	o	■	■	p	■	a	■	o
n	o	u	s	■	a	i	n	s	i
e	■	l	■	■	c	■	g	■	n
r	é	e	l	l	e	m	e	n	t

No. 14

p	a	s	s	e	p	o	r	t	s
o	■	t	■	■	a	■	a	■	a
i	l	y	a	■	s	e	n	t	i
n	■	l	■	■	s	■	g	■	s
t	r	o	u	p	e	■	■	■	i
d	■	■	■	a	r	a	b	e	s
e	■	a	■	q	■	■	o	■	s
v	o	u	l	u	■	d	i	r	a
u	■	r	■	e	■	■	r	■	n
e	x	a	c	t	e	m	e	n	t

No. 15

a	o	û	t	■	c	a	n	a	l
v	■	■	o	■	r	■	o	■	u
a	u	m	i	l	i	e	u	■	x
i	■	o	■	i	■	■	v	u	e
t	o	n	■	r	i	v	e	■	■
■	■	t	u	e	r	■	l	a	c
s	û	r	■	■	a	■	l	■	ô
e	■	a	r	r	i	v	e	n	t
i	■	i	■	u	■	i	■	■	e
n	o	t	r	e	■	f	a	i	s

No. 16

m	e	r	■	m	e	n	a	c	e
o	■	e	■	o	■	■	p	■	s
m	a	n	q	u	a	i	e	n	t
e	■	c	■	s	■	■	r	■	■
n	■	o	■	s	o	u	c	i	s
t	e	n	t	e	r	■	e	■	o
■	■	t	■	■	a	■	v	■	l
p	e	r	s	o	n	n	a	g	e
a	■	e	■	■	g	■	i	■	i
s	o	r	t	i	e	■	t	e	l

No. 17

a	r	m	é	e	■	m	a	i	s
v	■	é	■	a	■	u	■	■	i
e	■	p	o	u	r	r	a	i	t
c	a	r	■	■	i	■	m	■	u
■	■	i	d	é	e	■	o	s	é
v	i	s	■	p	n	e	u	■	■
a	■	e	■	é	■	■	r	o	i
c	e	r	v	e	l	l	e	■	v
h	■	■	i	■	i	■	u	■	r
e	l	l	e	■	t	e	x	t	e

No. 18

c	h	a	u	s	s	e	t	t	e
h	■	b	■	o	■	■	r	■	n
a	u	r	a	i	■	h	a	u	t
r	■	i	■	r	■	■	h	■	r
r	■	■	■	é	c	r	i	r	e
e	n	t	r	e	r	■	■	■	t
t	■	i	■	■	o	■	l	■	i
t	i	r	e	■	i	m	a	g	e
e	■	e	■	■	r	■	i	■	n
s	e	r	v	i	e	t	t	e	s

Solutions

No. 19

p	l	e	u	r	a	n	t		e
	o		n		s		a	n	s
a	i	s	e		s	o	n		p
p		u			u		t	h	é
p	a	r	l	e	r				r
e				m	e	t	t	r	a
l	i	é		p			u		i
a		g	e	l		v	e	n	t
i	r	a		o		a		o	
t		l	a	i	s	s	e	n	t

No. 20

t	r	o	u	v	e	r			i
	i		s		n		f	i	n
	t	h	é	â	t	r	e		s
à		é			ê		n	e	t
l	i	s	a	i	t		ê		a
a		i		m	e	n	t	o	n
m	o	t		i			r		t
o		e	n	t	r	é	e	s	
d	u	r		e		l		e	
e			t	r	o	u	b	l	é

No. 21

a	r	r	ê	t	d	e	b	u	s
b		a		r			l		u
a	n	n	é	e		p	o	u	r
n		g		n			n		l
d				t	e	n	d	r	e
o	f	f	r	e	s				p
n		e			p		a		o
n	o	m	s		a	i	n	s	i
e		m			c		g		n
r	é	e	l	l	e	m	e	n	t

No. 22

s	u	d		h	e	u	r	e	s
a		é		u			e		û
i	n	t	é	r	e	s	s	e	r
s		e		l			s		
o		r		e	f	f	e	t	s
n	o	m	b	r	e		m		o
		i			r		b		u
c	o	n	s	e	i	l	l	e	r
e		e			e		e		c
s	e	r	i	e	z		r	u	e

No. 23

		é	t	a	b	l	i	t	
l	i	t		n		i		o	
a		a	m	i		s	o	i	e
v	i	t		m			i		n
e				a	r	g	e	n	t
r	e	m	p	l	i				e
i		a			s		b	o	n
e	l	l	e		q	u	e		d
	a		a		u		c	a	s
	s	o	u	p	e	r	s		

No. 24

		s	t	a	t	u	e	s	
o	n	t		v		n		o	
b		y		a	p	p	e	l	s
s	e	l	o	n		e			e
e		o		c	o	u	r	i	r
r	e	s	t	e	r		é		v
v			r		d	i	g	n	e
é	c	l	a	i	r		l		n
	o		h		e		e	s	t
	l	a	i	s	s	e	r		

Solutions

No. 25

	b	a	t	t	a	i	t		
	o		h		s		a	n	s
a	l	l	é		s	o	n		o
r		e			a		t	e	l
r	é	s	o	l	u				e
i				é	t	a	b	l	i
v	i	f		z			a		l
é		i	r	a		p	l	i	s
e	u	x		r		a		c	
		e	n	d	o	r	m	i	

No. 26

	é	c	h	a	r	p	e		
	l		a		e		n	e	t
a	u	p	r	è	s		f		h
c			d		t	r	a	c	é
c	r	o	i	r	e		c		â
o		u		a	s	p	e	c	t
r	ê	v	e	s		o			r
d		e		o	c	c	u	p	e
s	u	r		i		h		u	
		t	e	r	r	e	u	r	

No. 27

t	a	r	d		b	l	o	n	d
a			o		a		r		o
p	i	a	n	i	s	t	e		i
i		c		d			i	l	s
s	e	c		é	g	a	l		
		o	s	e	r		l	a	c
n	o	m			e		e		a
o		p	r	o	c	u	r	e	r
i		l		s		s			t
r	u	i	n	é		é	p	é	e

No. 28

r	é	p	u	b	l	i	q	u	e
é		e			e		u		n
c	e	n	t		q	u	a	r	t
i		d			u		i		r
p	o	u	s	s	e				e
i				a	l	l	a	i	t
e		b		m			v		i
n	e	i	g	e		m	i	n	e
t		e		d			o		n
s	e	n	t	i	m	e	n	t	s

No. 29

s	a	i	s	o	n		m	o	t
u		n			u		a		e
d	é	t	e	r	m	i	n	e	r
		e			é		q		m
p	a	r	l	e	r		u		e
e		r		r	o	m	a	n	s
n		o		r			i		
c	o	m	m	e	n	c	e	n	t
h		p		u			n		u
é	m	u		r	e	n	t	r	é

No. 30

		d	é	f	e	n	s	e	
p	e	u		a		o		s	
i		r	o	i		n	o	t	e
l	i	é		b			u		n
o				l	a	p	i	n	s
t	o	m	b	e	r				u
e		o			b		l	u	i
s	o	i	f		r	u	e		t
	n		o		e		u	n	e
	t	o	u	s	s	e	r		

Solutions

No. 31

a	m	o	u	r	s		v	i	t
i		c			o		o		y
r	e	c	u	e	i	l	l	i	r
		u			r		o		a
o	p	p	o	s	é		n		n
u		a		t	e	x	t	e	s
v		i		y			i		
r	é	e	l	l	e	m	e	n	t
i		n		o			r		ô
r	i	t		s	a	i	s	i	t

No. 32

é	l	è	v	e	s		d	u	r
t			i		u		e		é
é	p	i	n	a	r	d	s		d
		n		g			c	o	u
c	a	s		i	v	r	e		i
l		t	i	r	e		n	e	t
i	r	a			u		d		
m		l	e	c	t	e	u	r	s
a		l		e		a			û
t	h	é		s	a	u	v	e	r

No. 33

p	r	é	s	e	n	t	e	n	t
h		v			a		l		e
a	f	i	n		v	o	l	e	r
r		e			i		e		r
m	a	r	i	e	r				i
a				f	e	r	a	i	t
c		b		f			u		o
i	m	a	g	e		v	r	a	i
e		n		t			a		r
n	é	c	e	s	s	a	i	r	e

No. 34

m	a	l	g	r	é		s	o	n
a			a		l		u		o
i	n	d	i	q	u	e	r		u
		i		u			p	a	r
m	i	s		o	s	e	r		r
e		a	m	i	e		i	c	i
t	o	i			n		s		
t		e	x	i	s	t	e	n	t
r		n		l		e			a
a	r	t		s	a	l	l	e	s

No. 35

n	o	v	e	m	b	r	e		e
	i		n		a		m	o	n
s	e	n	t		l		p		c
a			r		c	a	l	m	e
n	u	m	é	r	o		o		i
g		o		a	n	c	i	e	n
l	a	m	e	s		a			t
o		e		o	c	c	u	p	e
t	o	n		i		h		u	
s		t	e	r	r	e	u	r	s

No. 36

a		p	l	a	i	s	a	n	t
v	u	e		s		i		o	
a		u		p		g	a	n	t
n	a	p	p	e		n			o
t		l		c	h	e	m	i	n
a	v	e	r	t	i		o		n
g			e		v	o	t	r	e
e	s	t	i	m	e		i		r
	u		n		r		f	e	r
a	d	r	e	s	s	e	s		e

Solutions

No. 37

a	v	e	u	■	q	u	a	n	d
v	■	■	n	■	u	■	u	■	e
r	ê	v	e	r	i	e	s	■	u
i	■	o	■	i	■	■	s	i	x
l	u	i	■	r	a	v	i	■	■
■	■	t	u	e	r	■	t	u	é
p	e	u	■	■	m	■	ô	■	l
e	■	r	e	m	e	t	t	r	e
r	■	e	■	u	■	ô	■	■	v
d	é	s	i	r	■	t	i	r	é

No. 38

a	u	r	o	n	s	■	v	i	s
i	■	e	■	■	u	■	o	■	e
r	e	c	u	e	i	l	l	i	r
■	■	o	■	■	v	■	o	■	r
t	o	m	b	e	r	■	n	■	e
r	■	m	■	s	e	n	t	i	r
o	■	a	■	p	■	■	i	■	■
m	o	n	t	r	a	i	e	n	t
p	■	d	■	i	■	■	r	■	u
é	t	é	■	t	r	i	s	t	e

No. 39

m	o	u	t	a	r	d	e	■	d
■	u	■	e	■	i	■	f	é	e
h	i	e	r	■	s	■	f	■	m
o	■	■	r	■	q	u	e	u	e
n	i	v	e	a	u	■	t	■	u
n	■	a	■	v	e	r	s	e	r
e	n	c	r	e	■	o	■	■	e
u	■	h	■	n	o	m	m	e	r
r	u	e	■	i	■	a	■	a	■
s	■	s	e	r	i	n	g	u	e

No. 40

p	u	i	s	s	a	n	c	e	s
o	■	m	■	■	v	■	e	■	a
i	r	a	i	■	a	u	r	a	i
n	■	g	■	■	l	■	f	■	s
t	r	e	n	t	e	■	■	■	i
d	■	■	■	a	r	a	b	e	s
e	■	s	■	n	■	■	a	■	s
v	i	e	n	t	■	i	l	y	a
u	■	r	■	ô	■	■	l	■	n
e	x	a	c	t	e	m	e	n	t

No. 41

s	û	r	■	m	e	n	a	c	e
e	■	é	■	a	■	■	p	■	s
r	a	p	i	d	e	m	e	n	t
o	■	u	■	a	■	■	r	■	■
n	■	b	■	m	a	r	c	h	e
s	a	l	l	e	s	■	e	■	n
■	■	i	■	■	i	■	v	■	n
m	a	q	u	i	l	l	a	g	e
a	■	u	■	■	e	■	i	■	m
l	u	e	u	r	s	■	t	o	i

No. 42

a	n	x	i	é	t	é	s	■	q
■	o	■	r	■	h	■	c	r	u
e	n	g	a	g	é	■	è	■	a
n	■	■	■	r	■	■	n	e	t
s	e	l	■	i	d	é	e	■	o
e	■	a	i	s	e	■	s	u	r
m	a	i	■	■	n	■	■	■	z
b	■	s	■	a	t	r	o	c	e
l	i	s	■	m	■	i	■	r	■
e	■	e	x	i	s	t	a	i	t

Solutions

No. 43

c	o	n	v	a	i	n	c	r	e
a	■	u	■	r	■	■	h	■	n
p	r	i	e	r	■	l	a	i	t
i	■	t	■	ê	■	■	u	■	r
t	■	■	■	t	e	n	d	r	e
a	n	c	i	e	n	■	■	■	t
i	■	r	■	■	f	■	é	■	i
n	o	i	x	■	a	u	t	r	e
e	■	e	■	■	c	■	a	■	n
s	e	r	v	i	e	t	t	e	s

No. 44

■	l	i	b	e	r	t	é	■	■
■	u	■	i	■	o	■	n	o	m
r	i	d	e	a	u	■	o	■	o
o	■	■	n	■	t	y	r	a	n
c	h	a	s	s	e	■	m	■	s
h	■	u	■	a	s	p	e	c	t
e	n	f	e	u	■	o	■	■	r
r	■	o	■	t	r	i	s	t	e
s	o	n	■	e	■	d	■	u	■
■	■	d	u	r	e	s	t	e	■

No. 45

■	f	a	v	o	r	i	s	■	■
■	i	■	i	■	o	■	u	s	é
p	l	u	s	■	m	o	i	■	l
l	■	n	■	■	p	■	t	u	é
a	v	e	n	i	r	■	■	■	m
i	■	■	■	m	e	m	b	r	e
s	o	l	■	i	■	■	o	■	n
i	■	o	n	t	■	p	l	a	t
r	o	i	■	e	■	a	■	n	■
■	■	s	u	r	p	r	i	s	■

No. 46

■	■	i	n	s	p	i	r	é	■
c	a	r	■	e	■	l	■	l	■
u	■	a	i	r	■	s	œ	u	r
i	c	i	■	r	■	■	i	■	a
s	■	■	■	e	m	p	l	o	i
s	o	m	b	r	e	■	■	■	s
e	■	e	■	■	n	■	o	u	i
s	o	r	t	■	t	o	n	■	n
■	i	■	a	■	o	■	d	é	s
■	e	s	s	e	n	c	e	■	■

No. 47

d	i	s	■	e	n	t	i	e	r
é	■	o	■	n	■	■	n	■	u
f	o	u	r	c	h	e	t	t	e
a	■	f	■	o	■	■	r	■	■
u	■	f	■	r	a	s	o	i	r
t	e	r	m	e	s	■	d	■	é
■	■	a	■	■	t	■	u	■	s
c	o	n	s	t	r	u	i	r	e
o	■	c	■	■	e	■	r	■	a
l	u	e	u	r	s	■	e	a	u

No. 48

p	a	r	f	u	m	■	l	i	é
a	■	e	■	■	e	■	a	■	t
s	e	c	r	é	t	a	i	r	e
■	■	o	■	■	t	■	s	■	i
t	o	m	b	e	r	■	s	■	n
r	■	m	■	s	e	r	a	i	t
o	■	a	■	p	■	■	i	■	■
m	o	n	t	r	a	i	e	n	t
p	■	d	■	i	■	■	n	■	ô
é	t	é	■	t	a	n	t	ô	t

Solutions

No. 49

c	e	s		f	a	u	t	e	s
o		e		a			e		u
c	o	n	s	i	d	é	r	e	r
h		t		b			r		
o		i		l	a	p	i	n	s
n	o	m	m	e	r		t		a
		e			r		o		i
f	a	n	t	a	i	s	i	e	s
é		t			v		r		i
e	s	s	a	y	é		e	s	t

No. 50

	s	o	m	m	e	i	l		
	û		a		s		a	m	i
p	r	e	n	d	s		v		n
a			g		a	v	a	n	t
s	a	m	e	d	i		b		é
s		i		e	s	p	o	i	r
a	p	r	è	s		o			ê
n		o		s	e	r	o	n	t
t	o	i		u		t		e	
		r	e	s	p	e	c	t	

No. 51

i	n	g	é	n	i	e	u	r	s
n		a		o			t		i
t	e	n	d	u		f	i	l	m
é		t		r			l		p
r				r	é	v	e	i	l
e	n	f	a	i	t				e
s		i			e		d		m
s	a	n	s		n	e	i	g	e
e		i			d		r		n
r	e	t	r	o	u	v	a	i	t

No. 52

		r	e	m	o	r	d	s	
f	o	u		o		o		e	
a		b		t	a	i	l	l	e
i	r	a			m				n
s		n	o	t	e		l	i	t
a	n	s		i	r	a	i		e
i				r			m	o	n
s	o	m	m	e	s		i		d
	s		e		o		t	a	s
	é	t	r	a	n	g	e		

No. 53

p	r	o	m	e	n	a	d	e	s
h		u			a		a		o
a	v	e	z		v	e	n	d	u
r		s			i		s		f
m	é	t	i	e	r				f
a				f	e	r	m	e	r
c		b		f			a		a
i	m	a	g	e		b	r	u	n
e		n		t			d		c
n	é	c	e	s	s	a	i	r	e

No. 54

a		d	e	r	e	t	o	u	r
c	o	u		e		a		n	
c		r		n	a	p	p	e	s
e	x	a	c	t		i			e
p		n		r	e	s	t	e	r
t	i	t	r	e	s		i		a
e			a		p	a	r	m	i
r	é	g	n	e	r		a		e
	l		g		i		n	o	n
a	u	s	s	i	t	ô	t		t

Solutions

No. 55

d	é	g	o	û	t		p	a	s
u		é			e		e		e
r	e	n	c	o	n	t	r	e	r
		é			d		m		v
s	o	r	t	i	r		e		i
o		a		m	e	n	t	i	r
m		t		i			t		
m	a	i	n	t	e	n	a	n	t
e		o		e			i		u
t	o	n		r	e	n	t	r	é

No. 56

c	e	s		m	é	p	r	i	s
o		e		o			é		u
c	o	n	d	u	c	t	e	u	r
h		t		s			l		
o		i		s	a	l	l	e	s
n	o	m	m	e	r		e		o
		e			g		m		r
f	i	n	a	l	e	m	e	n	t
i		t			n		n		i
l	i	s	a	i	t		t	u	e

No. 57

a		p	r	e	s	s	i	o	n
g	a	i		s		e		u	
i		e		t		n	o	i	r
s	e	r	a	i		t			e
s		r		m	a	i	s	o	n
a	m	e	n	e	r		e		t
i			u		d	î	n	e	r
t	o	m	a	t	e		t		a
	i		g		u		i	c	i
d	e	m	e	u	r	e	r		t

No. 58

f	l	a	m	m	e		a		f
	i		o		s		g	e	l
r	é	s	i	s	t	e	r		e
		o		o			é	m	u
e	a	u		i	l	y	a		r
n		l	i	e	u		b	a	s
v	i	e			n		l		
e		v	i	v	e	m	e	n	t
r	u	e		u		o		o	
s		r		e	n	n	e	m	i

No. 59

c	o	u	r	i	r		p	a	r
a		n			e		h		e
s	a	i	s	i	s	s	a	n	t
		v			t		r		i
p	l	e	u	r	e		m		r
e		r		e	s	s	a	y	é
n		s		v			c		
c	h	i	r	u	r	g	i	e	s
h		t		e			e		û
é	t	é		s	o	n	n	e	r

No. 60

a	p	p	a	r	e	n	c	e	s
s		e			s		h		u
c	e	r	f		p	l	o	m	b
e		d			r		u		i
n	o	u	r	r	i				t
s				é	t	o	i	l	e
e		f		v			m		m
u	t	i	l	e		f	a	c	e
r		l		i			g		n
s	i	m	p	l	e	m	e	n	t

Solutions

No. 61

p	l	a	i	n	t	e	s		m
	o		l		o		a	m	i
f	i	l	s		m	a	i		l
r		a			b		s	e	l
a	s	s	u	r	e				i
p				a	r	r	i	v	e
p	a	s		i			r		r
a		a	n	s		m	a	r	s
n	o	n		i		a		i	
t		s	a	n	g	l	o	t	s

No. 62

r	e	c	u	e	i	l	l	i	r
é		r			n		o		é
p	e	u	x		f	a	i	r	e
u		e			i		n		l
b	a	l	l	o	n				l
l				f	i	è	v	r	e
i		s		f			o		m
q	u	e	u	e		v	i	t	e
u		r		r			l		n
e	x	a	c	t	e	m	e	n	t

No. 63

c	a	t	h	é	d	r	a	l	e
h		o		t			u		n
a	v	i	d	e		p	r	ê	t
r		t		i			a		r
r				n	a	v	i	r	e
e	f	f	e	t	s				t
t		i			p		a		i
t	e	n	u		e	n	v	i	e
e		i			c		e		n
s	e	r	v	i	t	e	u	r	s

No. 64

a	p	p	a	r	a	î	t	r	e
u		e			l		u		n
p	e	u	t		l	u	e	u	r
a		r			u		r		e
r	e	s	t	e	r				v
a				m	e	t	t	r	a
v		ô		p			r		n
a	u	t	e	l		b	a	n	c
n		e		o			h		h
t	e	r	r	i	t	o	i	r	e

No. 65

c	o	u	v	r	a	i	t		a
	i		e		u		a	r	t
s	e	r	r	e	r		i		t
e			r		a	l	l	é	e
m	ê	m	e	s	i		l		n
b		e		a	t	t	e	n	d
l	u	n	d	i		o			r
a		t		s	e	m	b	l	e
i	c	i		o		b		i	
t		r	e	n	v	e	r	s	é

No. 66

p	l	u	s		v	i	e	n	s
o			o		a		x		o
n	o	b	l	e	s	s	e		i
t		a		l			m	e	r
s	u	r		l	o	u	p		
		r	i	e	n		l	i	é
f	é	e			z		e		c
a		a	d	r	e	s	s	e	r
i		u		u		o			i
t	e	x	t	e		n	u	i	t

Solutions

No. 67

d	a	n	g	e	r	■	p	a	r
u	■	■	a	■	o	■	r	■	e
r	a	p	i	d	i	t	é	■	n
■	■	r	■	i	■	■	s	u	d
t	h	é	■	r	i	v	e	■	e
i	■	c	i	e	l	■	n	e	z
t	o	i	■	■	y	■	t	■	■
r	■	e	n	f	a	c	e	d	e
e	■	u	■	e	■	e	■	■	a
s	i	x	■	r	é	s	e	a	u

No. 68

■	■	s	a	v	a	n	t	s	■
p	e	u	■	i	■	o	■	û	■
o	■	b	u	t	■	m	a	r	i
m	o	i	■	r	■	■	i	■	n
p	■	■	■	e	s	p	r	i	t
i	m	p	o	s	é	■	■	■	é
e	■	u	■	■	p	■	c	a	r
r	i	r	e	■	a	m	i	■	ê
■	r	■	u	■	r	■	t	ô	t
■	a	n	x	i	é	t	é	■	■

No. 69

c	o	n	v	a	i	n	c	r	e
a	■	i	■	s	■	■	h	■	n
p	n	e	u	s	■	t	a	n	t
i	■	r	■	u	■	■	u	■	r
t	■	■	■	r	e	n	d	r	e
a	n	c	i	e	n	■	■	■	t
i	■	r	■	■	f	■	d	■	i
n	o	i	r	■	a	s	i	l	e
e	■	e	■	■	i	■	e	■	n
s	e	r	v	i	t	e	u	r	s

No. 70

d	o	s	■	c	o	u	s	i	n
e	■	e	■	a	■	■	a	■	o
m	é	c	a	n	i	c	i	e	n
ê	■	r	■	a	■	■	s	■	■
m	■	é	■	p	l	a	i	r	a
e	n	t	r	é	e	■	s	■	m
■	■	a	■	■	ç	■	s	■	i
c	l	i	g	n	o	t	a	n	t
o	■	r	■	■	n	■	n	■	i
l	u	e	u	r	s	■	t	u	é

No. 71

■	m	é	d	e	c	i	n	■	■
■	a	■	a	■	h	■	o	u	i
v	i	a	n	d	e	■	u	■	n
i	■	■	s	■	m	è	r	e	s
s	a	m	e	d	i	■	r	■	p
i	■	e	■	i	n	f	i	n	i
t	e	n	i	r	■	e	■	■	r
e	■	a	■	a	r	r	i	v	é
s	e	c	■	i	■	a	■	i	■
■	■	e	n	s	u	i	t	e	■

No. 72

f	e	r	o	n	t	■	c	a	s
o	■	e	■	■	e	■	o	■	e
i	n	t	e	r	r	o	m	p	u
■	■	o	■	■	m	■	p	■	i
m	o	u	s	s	e	■	t	■	l
e	■	r	■	e	s	s	a	i	s
n	■	n	■	r	■	■	b	■	■
t	r	a	v	a	i	l	l	e	r
o	■	n	■	i	■	■	e	■	i
n	e	t	■	s	a	i	s	i	t

Solutions

No. 73

	p	l	a	i	s	i	r		
	l		n		a		o	s	é
p	u	i	s		l	u	i		g
i		c			u		s	o	l
l	a	i	s	s	e				i
o				a	r	a	b	e	s
t	o	n		u			a		e
e		o	n	t		p	l	u	s
s	u	r		e		a		n	
		d	u	r	e	s	t	e	

No. 74

h	o	r	r	i	b	l	e		d
	i		e		a		f	é	e
c	e	c	i		r		f		m
o			n		q	u	e	u	e
n	i	v	e	a	u		t		u
s		i		v	e	r	s	e	r
e	n	t	r	e		o			e
r		r		n	o	m	m	e	r
v	u	e		i		a		a	
é		s	e	r	i	n	g	u	e

No. 75

b	o	l	s		p	l	a	c	é
l			e		e		s		t
a	i	l	l	e	u	r	s		é
n		o		l			i	l	s
c	r	i		l	i	m	e		
		n	i	e	r		t	o	i
t	ô	t			a		t		r
r		a	r	r	i	v	e	r	a
è		i		u		i			i
s	i	n	g	e		f	o	n	t

No. 76

m	a	r	q	u	é		c	e	s
o		e			l		a		o
i	n	t	é	r	e	s	s	e	r
		r			v		q		t
b	r	o	s	s	e		u		i
o		u		e	r	r	e	u	r
u		v		r			t		
c	h	a	r	r	e	t	t	e	s
h		i		e			e		o
e	s	t		r	a	i	s	i	n

No. 77

a	r	r	ê	t	d	e	b	u	s
b		a		r			l		u
a	n	n	é	e		c	o	u	r
n		g		n			n		l
d				t	e	n	d	r	e
o	f	f	r	e	s				p
n		a			p		a		o
n	u	i	t		a	i	n	s	i
e		r			c		g		n
r	é	e	l	l	e	m	e	n	t

No. 78

d	i	s		b	a	l	l	o	n
u		a		e			a		o
c	h	i	r	u	r	g	i	e	n
o		s		r			s		
u		i		r	a	i	s	o	n
p	a	s	s	e	r		a		a
		s			d		i		î
c	h	a	n	g	e	m	e	n	t
a		n			u		n		r
r	e	t	o	u	r		t	u	e

Solutions

No. 79

d	é	s		c	h	a	c	u	n
é		o		e			h		e
p	o	u	r	r	a	i	e	n	t
o		p		i			v		
s		ç		s	a	v	a	i	s
é	c	o	l	e	s		l		e
		n			s		i		n
m	a	n	q	u	a	i	e	n	t
i		e			u		r		i
s	e	r	o	n	t		s	û	r

No. 80

r	a	p	p	o	r	t	s		j
	i		a		e		u	n	e
p	r	i	s		i	c	i		u
r		r			n		t	o	n
o	r	a	n	g	e				e
b				e	s	s	a	i	s
l	i	s		n			m		s
è		o	n	t		r	i	v	e
m	a	i		i		o		i	
e		f	a	l	a	i	s	e	s

No. 81

d	o	u	b	l	e		m	e	r
o		n			x		é		a
n	a	i	s	s	a	n	c	e	s
		v			m		a		o
p	l	e	u	r	e		n		i
e		r		e	n	t	i	e	r
n		s		v			c		
c	h	i	r	u	r	g	i	e	s
h		t		e			e		u
é	t	é		s	o	n	n	e	r

No. 82

		p	r	o	d	u	i	t	
e	a	u		i		s		u	
n		i	l	s		é	p	é	e
c	a	s		e			e		n
o				a	c	q	u	i	s
u	n	j	o	u	r				u
r		e			i		g	a	i
s	o	u	s		m	u	r		t
	s		e		e		o	i	e
	é	g	l	i	s	e	s		

No. 83

		c	o	m	p	t	e	s	
c	r	u		u		i		o	
é		i		s	e	r	o	n	s
l	i	v	r	é		e			o
è		r		e	r	r	e	u	r
b	l	e	s	s	é		f		t
r			h		s	u	f	f	i
e	n	v	o	i	e		e		e
	o		r		a		t	a	s
	m	o	t	e	u	r	s		

No. 84

a		n	o	b	l	e	s	s	e
p	l	u		u		n		i	
e		a		r		f	i	x	é
r	è	g	l	e		e			t
ç		e		a	t	r	o	c	e
o	b	s	c	u	r		f		r
i			h		e	n	f	i	n
t	é	m	o	i	n		e		u
	l		s		t		r	u	e
j	u	g	e	m	e	n	t		r

Solutions

No. 85

v	e	r	r	e		b	é	b	é
u		é		s		e			c
e		a	t	t	a	c	h	e	r
s	o	l			m		a		i
		i	r	a	i		b	u	t
l	a	s		c	e	c	i		
a		e		t			l	i	t
p	a	r	c	e	q	u	e		r
i			a		u		t		è
n	o	i	r		i	d	é	e	s

No. 86

	d	é	l	i	c	a	t		
	u		i		h		o	u	i
p	r	è	s	d	e		u		n
a			t		m	a	r	i	s
s	a	m	e	d	i		n		p
s		i		e	n	n	e	m	i
a	b	r	i	s		a			r
i		o		s	é	p	a	r	é
t	o	i		u		p		i	
		r	e	s	p	e	c	t	

No. 87

s	u	d		v	o	y	a	i	s
a		é		e			s		û
i	n	t	é	r	e	s	s	e	r
s		e		s			u		
o		r		e	s	p	r	i	t
n	o	m	b	r	e		é		a
		i			r		m		n
m	a	n	q	u	a	i	e	n	t
o		e			i		n		ô
t	i	r	a	i	t		t	ô	t

No. 88

		p	r	o	d	u	i	t	
f	e	u		r		n		e	
l		i	r	a		e	l	l	e
a	n	s		n			a		n
m				g	a	u	c	h	e
m	i	l	i	e	u				f
e		u			r		v	i	f
s	a	i	t		a	m	i		e
	r		h		i		d	i	t
	t	h	é	â	t	r	e		

No. 89

c	i	t	r	o	u	i	l	l	e
h		u		p			a		s
a	m	e	n	é		t	r	o	p
r		r		r			g		é
r				e	r	r	e	u	r
e	s	p	è	r	e				a
t		r			n		s		n
t	o	i	t		t	r	o	n	c
e		e			r		r		e
s	e	r	v	i	e	t	t	e	s

No. 90

e			s	e	r	v	a	i	t
m	e	r		n		i		l	
p		e	n	f	a	n	t	s	
o	n	t		a			r		a
r		e		c	a	p	o	t	s
t	e	n	t	e	r		u		s
é		i			r		v	i	e
	o	r	i	g	i	n	e		o
	s		c		v		r	o	i
m	é	r	i	t	e	r			r

Solutions

No. 91

p		a	i	g	u	i	l	l	e
é	m	u		â		r		i	
r		r		t	r	a	i	t	s
i	m	a	g	e		i			e
o		i		a	c	t	e	u	r
d	è	s	q	u	e		f		a
e			u		s	u	f	f	i
s	e	r	a	i	s		e		e
	a		r		e		t	o	n
g	u	i	t	a	r	e	s		t

No. 92

a	u	f	a	i	t		s	o	l
i		i			u		e		i
r	e	n	c	o	n	t	r	e	s
		a			n		v		a
v	a	l	l	é	e		i		i
o		e		p	l	u	t	ô	t
l		m		i			e		
c	h	e	r	c	h	e	u	r	s
a		n		e			r		u
n	e	t		s	a	i	s	i	r

No. 93

r		e	n	t	r	a	î	n	é
a	u	x		r		i		o	
p		p		o		m	è	n	e
p	e	r	d	u		e			n
o		è		p	a	r	e	n	t
r	e	s	t	e	r		s		e
t			y		m	a	t	i	n
é	c	a	r	t	é		i		d
	r		a		e		m	u	r
p	i	a	n	i	s	t	e		e

No. 94

é	t	é		f	e	r	m	e	s
v		c		i			a		o
i	n	o	n	d	a	t	i	o	n
e		n		è			n		
r		o		l	a	i	t	u	e
s	o	m	m	e	s		e		n
		i			i		n		n
m	a	q	u	i	l	l	a	g	e
a		u			e		n		m
l	u	e	u	r	s		t	o	i

No. 95

p	o	u	s	s	e	t	t	e	s
e		t			n		e		e
n	u	i	t		v	e	n	i	r
d		l			o		u		v
a	v	e	r	t	i				i
n				r	e	n	t	r	e
t		v		i			i		t
q	u	a	i	s		é	t	a	t
u		u		t			r		e
e	n	t	r	e	t	i	e	n	s

No. 96

m	o	t	s		c	l	e	f	s
a			û		r		x		o
r	e	t	r	o	u	v	e		n
i		o		n			m	e	t
n	o	m		d	r	a	p		
		b	l	e	u		l	i	s
f	é	e			d		e		e
o		a	d	r	e	s	s	e	r
n		u		u		u			a
t	e	x	t	e		d	o	i	s

Solutions

No. 97

m	a	i		g	o	u	t	t	e
a		n		l			r		s
r	e	t	r	o	u	v	a	i	t
q		é		i			v		
u		r		r	o	m	a	n	s
é	l	e	v	e	r		i		a
		s			d		l		i
c	a	s	s	e	r	o	l	e	s
o		e			e		e		i
l	a	r	m	e	s		r	i	t

No. 98

	d	e	s	c	e	n	d		
	u		i		s		o	u	i
p	r	i	x		p	e	u		n
u		c			è		é	l	u
b	a	i	s	e	r				t
l				r	e	m	p	l	i
i	r	a		r			u		l
e		v	i	e		p	r	i	e
r	o	i		u		a		l	
		s	u	r	p	r	i	s	

No. 99

a	g	r	é	a	b	l	e		a
	a		t		a		m	o	n
d	i	e	u		s		p		t
o			d		s	a	l	l	e
m	ê	m	e	s	i		o		n
i		e		a	n	c	i	e	n
c	o	n	ç	u		h			e
i		a		t	r	o	n	c	s
l	o	i		e		s		a	
e		t	e	r	r	e	u	r	s

No. 100

p	l	a	n	t	é		c	a	s
a		b			p		h		i
s	h	a	m	p	o	o	i	n	g
		n			q		r		n
c	a	d	e	a	u		u		e
o		o		r	e	p	r	i	s
r		n		r			g		
d	e	n	t	i	f	r	i	c	e
e		e		v			e		a
s	u	r		é	t	e	n	d	u

No. 101

		s	é	j	o	u	r	s	
v	u	e		o		n		e	
e		p	l	u		e	l	l	e
n	e	t		e			i		n
t				n	a	î	t	r	e
r	é	c	i	t	s				f
e		r			s		v	i	f
s	a	i	t		a	m	i		e
	r		h		u		d	i	t
	t	h	é	â	t	r	e		

No. 102

j	u	s		p	o	u	r	r	a
u		e		r			é		i
s	u	c	c	e	s	s	e	u	r
q		r		s			l		
u		é		s	t	y	l	o	s
e	n	t	r	é	e		e		o
		a			n		m		r
l	a	i	s	s	a	i	e	n	t
i		r			i		n		i
é	t	e	i	n	t		t	u	e

Solutions

No. 103

		e	s	t	o	m	a	c	
l	a	s		e		o		o	
i		p		l	a	i	t	u	e
m	u	r			v				n
i		i	v	r	e		m	e	t
t	ô	t		a	c	t	e		e
e				v			n	o	n
s	o	u	m	i	s		a		d
	s		e		o		c	r	u
	é	t	r	a	n	g	e		

No. 104

p	r	o	p	r	i	é	t	é	s
a		u		é			o		u
n	e	r	f	s		f	u	i	r
t		s		o			r		l
o				l	a	i	s	s	e
u	n	j	o	u	r				p
f		e			a		i		o
l	o	u	p		b	a	l	a	i
e		d			e		y		n
s	a	i	s	i	s	s	a	n	t

No. 105

p	a	r		m	a	l	a	d	e
o		e		o			p		s
m	a	n	q	u	a	i	e	n	t
m		c		s			r		
e		o		s	o	u	c	i	s
s	o	n	g	e	r		e		a
		t			a		v		m
p	e	r	s	o	n	n	a	g	e
u		e			g		i		d
r	i	s	q	u	e		t	o	i

No. 106

a	t	t	i	r	é		m	a	l
n		o			p		o		a
s	o	u	p	ç	o	n	n	e	r
		t			q		t		m
c	a	d	e	a	u		r		e
o		a		s	e	r	a	i	s
u		b		p			i		
p	r	o	f	e	s	s	e	u	r
e		r		c			n		i
s	u	d		t	a	n	t	ô	t

No. 107

p	r	é	f	é	r	é			p
	o		e		e		l	u	i
	i	n	u	t	i	l	e		e
g		a			n		c	a	r
a	r	r	i	v	e		t		r
r		i		a	s	s	u	r	e
d	o	n		l			r		s
a		e	n	l	e	v	e	r	
i	l	s		é		i		u	
t			d	e	r	n	i	e	r

No. 108

m	o	t	s		f	l	o	t	s
a			u		o		r		u
r	e	t	r	a	i	t	e		b
d		r		b			i	c	i
i	r	a		r	é	e	l		
		v	o	i	t		l	a	c
v	i	e			é		e		a
é		r	a	s	s	u	r	e	r
l		s		û		s			t
o	b	é	i	r		é	p	é	e

Solutions

No. 109

f	o	r	c	e		f	i	l	s
é		é		a		e			i
e		f	a	u	d	r	a	i	t
s	e	l			e		n		u
		é	g	a	l		t	h	é
s	e	c		g	a	r	e		
a		h		i			n	o	m
l	o	i	n	t	a	i	n		ê
u			e		i		e		m
t	o	i	t		r	e	s	t	e

No. 110

p	h	a	r	m	a	c	i	e	n
a		b		e			r		o
s	u	b	i	t		p	a	r	u
s		é		t			i		r
e				r	e	s	t	e	r
p	a	t	t	e	s				i
o		i			p		p		t
r	i	r	e		a	d	i	e	u
t		e			c		e		r
s	u	r	p	r	e	n	d	r	e

No. 111

a		p	r	e	s	s	i	o	n
v	u	e		n		u		u	
a		u		n		f	a	i	m
n	a	p	p	e		f			a
ç		l		m	a	i	s	o	n
a	v	e	n	i	r		e		g
i			e		d	o	u	z	e
t	o	u	r	n	e		i		a
	i		f		u		l	o	i
r	e	s	s	o	r	t	s		t

No. 112

		m	é	d	e	c	i	n	
p	l	u		i		r		o	
i		s		t	o	u	r	n	é
l	i	é			s				g
o		e	l	l	e		t	e	l
t	a	s		i	r	a	i		i
e				m			m	i	s
s	o	m	m	e	s		i		e
	s		e		o		d	é	s
	é	t	r	a	n	g	e		

No. 113

a	n	s		b	a	n	a	n	e
p		o		u			p		s
p	o	u	r	r	a	i	e	n	t
e		p		e			r		
l		ç		a	v	o	c	a	t
é	p	o	q	u	e		e		a
		n			r		v		n
c	o	n	c	e	r	n	a	n	t
o		e			e		i		ô
l	a	r	m	e	s		t	ô	t

No. 114

à			o	r	a	g	e	u	x
d	u	r		a		a		n	
r		e	x	p	r	i	m	e	
o	n	t		i			i		o
i		e		d	o	n	n	e	r
t	e	n	t	e	r		u		e
e		i			a		t	o	i
	c	r	a	i	n	t	e		l
	a		m		g		s	o	l
a	r	r	i	v	e	r			e

Solutions

No. 115

p	a	r	■	a	v	o	u	e	r
e	■	é	■	s	■	■	n	■	u
n	é	c	e	s	s	a	i	r	e
s	■	i	■	u	■	■	v	■	■
e	■	p	■	r	e	j	e	t	é
r	e	i	n	e	s	■	r	■	t
■	■	e	■	■	s	■	s	■	e
g	é	n	é	r	a	t	i	o	n
e	■	t	■	■	i	■	t	■	d
l	i	s	t	e	s	■	é	m	u

No. 116

r	ê	v	e	r	■	j	u	g	é
é	■	é	■	o	■	u	■	■	c
e	■	r	u	i	s	s	e	a	u
l	u	i	■	■	e	■	n	■	m
■	■	f	e	r	a	■	f	é	e
f	o	i	■	a	u	r	a	■	■
â	■	e	■	c	■	■	c	e	s
c	e	r	v	e	l	l	e	■	u
h	■	■	i	■	a	■	d	■	i
é	t	a	t	■	c	l	e	f	s

No. 117

c	o	n	t	i	n	u	a	n	t
a	■	o	■	m	■	■	u	■	e
s	e	r	a	i	■	ô	t	e	r
s	■	d	■	t	■	■	e	■	r
e	■	■	■	e	m	p	l	o	i
r	o	m	p	r	e	■	■	■	t
o	■	e	■	■	t	■	t	■	o
l	o	n	g	■	t	r	a	h	i
e	■	e	■	■	r	■	r	■	r
s	u	r	p	r	e	n	d	r	e

No. 118

p	o	c	h	e	■	s	o	n	s
l	■	a	■	a	■	û	■	■	i
i	■	p	o	u	r	r	a	i	t
s	u	r	■	■	i	■	t	■	u
■	■	i	v	r	e	■	t	h	é
b	e	c	■	a	n	g	e	■	■
l	■	e	■	v	■	■	n	e	z
a	u	s	s	i	t	ô	t	■	è
n	■	■	e	■	o	■	a	■	l
c	i	e	l	■	n	o	t	r	e

No. 119

c	o	n	v	a	i	n	c	r	e
o	■	o	■	b	■	■	r	■	n
m	a	i	n	s	■	t	o	u	t
p	■	x	■	e	■	■	i	■	r
t	■	■	■	n	a	î	t	r	e
a	b	a	t	t	u	■	■	■	t
b	■	c	■	■	r	■	b	■	i
l	o	i	s	■	a	l	l	é	e
e	■	e	■	■	i	■	e	■	n
s	e	r	v	i	t	e	u	r	s

No. 120

p	r	o	p	r	i	é	t	é	s
a	■	u	■	é	■	■	r	■	u
n	e	r	f	s	■	p	o	u	r
t	■	s	■	o	■	■	u	■	l
o	■	■	■	l	a	i	s	s	e
u	n	j	o	u	r	■	■	■	p
f	■	e	■	■	a	■	i	■	o
l	o	u	p	■	b	a	l	a	i
e	■	d	■	■	e	■	y	■	n
s	a	i	s	i	s	s	a	n	t

Solutions

No. 121

		f	a	l	a	i	s	e	
m	a	i		e		r		s	
é		g		t	r	a	i	t	s
c	o	u	r	t		i			o
h		r		r	e	t	e	n	u
a	m	e	n	e	r		n		v
n			u		r	i	c	h	e
t	i	m	i	d	e		o		n
	r		t		u		r	i	t
	a	b	s	u	r	d	e		

No. 122

a		c	o	n	d	a	m	n	é
v	u	e		o		n		o	
a		n	o	m		s	a	n	g
n	e	t		b			r		a
ç				r	e	s	t	e	r
a	n	c	i	e	n				a
i		a			v		v	i	n
t	o	r	t		a	m	i		t
	u		ô		i		t	o	i
d	i	s	t	a	n	c	e		r

No. 123

d	é	p	o	s	é		o	i	e
o		u			p		c		s
n	a	i	s	s	a	n	c	e	s
		s			u		u		a
p	a	s	m	a	l		p		i
a		a		s	e	r	a	i	s
r		n		i			i		
f	a	c	i	l	e	m	e	n	t
u		e		e			n		u
m	i	s		s	o	r	t	i	e

No. 124

e		c	e	i	n	t	u	r	e
s	o	l		l		e		u	
c		o		s	a	l	l	e	s
l	a	c			c				e
a		h	u	i	t		s	o	n
v	i	e		d	e	l	a		t
e				é			m	o	i
s	o	m	m	e	s		e		e
	s		a		e		d	u	r
r	é	f	l	é	c	h	i		s

No. 125

p	r	é	s	e	n	t	e	n	t
h		v			a		l		e
a	g	i	t		v	o	l	e	r
r		e			i		e		r
m	a	r	i	e	r				i
a				f	e	r	a	i	t
c		b		f			u		o
i	m	a	g	e		i	r	a	i
e		n		t			a		r
n	é	c	e	s	s	a	i	r	e

Made in the USA
Middletown, DE
07 November 2020

23497963R00084